# The Difference Is You:

## Power Through Positive Leadership

Mel Hawkins

Copyright © 2013 Mel Hawkins

All rights reserved.

ISBN: 1493739433
ISBN 13: 9781493739431

## Note from the Author

*Originally written in 1990, this work was revised in 1998. It has been edited for proofing purposes, only, prior to this publication release in 2013. The world has changed since 1990 and 1998 but the principles of positive leadership are timeless.*

*My thanks to Ryan G. Wilson for the cover design.*

## Other books by this author:

*Radical Surgery: Reconstructing the American Health Care System,* 1stBooksLibrary, 2002

*Light and Transient Causes,* a novel, a Kindle book, published in 2013.

*Reinventing Education, Hope, and the American Dream: The Challenge for Twenty-First Century America,* a Kindle book published in 2013.

## Contents

| | |
|---|---|
| PART I - AN INTRODUCTION TO POSITIVE LEADERSHIP | IX |
| ONE - THE ROLE OF LEADERSHIP | 1 |
| TWO - THE POSITIVE PRINCIPLE | 27 |
| THREE - THE GIFT OF SUCCESS | 43 |
| PART II - ATTRIBUTES OF POSITIVE LEADERS | 59 |
| FOUR - A HEALTHY SELF-ESTEEM | 61 |
| FIVE - UNDERSTANDS ORGANIZATIONS | 97 |
| SIX - COMMITMENT TO MISSION, VISION, AND VALUES | 137 |
| SEVEN - UNDERSTANDS THAT SUCCESS IS A PROCESS | 171 |
| EIGHT - UNDERSTANDS MOTIVATION | 189 |
| PART III - THINGS YOU CAN DO! | 205 |
| NINE - ACTION PLANS AND PROPOSALS | 207 |

TEN - ACTION STRATEGIES FOR HOME,

FAMILY, AND COMMUNITY 211

ABOUT THE AUTHOR 237

# PART I - AN INTRODUCTION TO POSITIVE LEADERSHIP

## *one*

## The Role Of Leadership

Are you happy with your job and with your career? Are you proud of your company and the people with whom you work? Do you feel like yours is a dead end job? Do you wish you worked somewhere exciting and challenging? Do you wonder if a break will ever come your way?

Do your supervisors respect you and recognize your efforts and contributions? Do they listen to you and ask for your input in tough situations? Do they give you the respect you feel you deserve? If you are a supervisor, how would your employees answer these questions about you?

Are you happy with your marriage? Is your spouse the kind of supportive partner you would like to have? Are your children turning out the way you hoped? Are your friends everything you want good friends to be?

Are you concerned about the direction in which our country is heading? Are you troubled by our nation's economic competitiveness in the world marketplace? Do you worry about the bureaucratic ineffectiveness of our government? Does the moral fiber of our society appear to be unraveling? Do you think our systems of education are adequately preparing our children for the future? Do you feel safe in your neighborhood at all hours of the day?

Do the myriad of problems confronting our society leave you feeling discouraged and helpless? If you are like millions of other men and women, discouraged and helpless is exactly how you feel but listen closely. *The Difference is You: Power Through Positive Leadership* is a message of hope.

The premise of this work is that there is much that we, as individuals, can do that will have an impact on the problems facing us in our personal lives, as a nation, and as citizens of the world community. The problems we face as a society, as we proceed through the Twenty-First Century, are functions of the quality of leadership of our human organizations.

Our message is simple. These problems, in all of their diversity and complexity, can be resolved thereby improving the quality of life for all human beings. Today's problems will be replaced by new problems, to be sure, but these, too, have solutions. In each case, solutions flow from effective leadership. What is new about this idea is the definition we assign to leadership and how far we spread its mantle.

Positive leadership is a special kind of leadership that gives individual men and women incredible power to bring about positive change and to make a difference right now, right where you are, at this moment in time!

**Now** is the best time to impact your organization and the job or role you now occupy is the right place to do it!

Many people put things off, waiting for the right or perfect time and place. Just as there are no perfect solutions, there is no perfect time and place. There is no time or place other than here and now. Do it now or, as they say in the athletic shoe commercial, "Just Do It!"

Now is always the best time for taking action and, the best opportunities are not the ones that fall into your lap but the ones you make for yourself. Do not delay another hour; begin anew. Start doing things differently. Take Zig Ziglar's advice:

"If you keep doin' what you've been doin', you're gonna keep gettin' what you've been gettin'."[1]

---

1   Ziglar, Zig, *See You At the Top*, Pelican Publishing Co., Gretna, LA, 1982.

Initiate changes in your life and in your approach to your duties, responsibilities, and your relationships and the world will begin to change in response. However small, even insignificant these changes may appear, they matter and they are the direct result of your leadership.

Be a positive leader in the same sense that you want the changes to be positive for everyone, whenever possible. Be concerned about values and begin thinking about the organization or community as a whole. Whatever the organizations of which you are a part, think about their purpose or mission and how you can best contribute to them. As you become more comfortable with your role as a leader, you will begin to see abundant opportunities to make an impact or to bring about change. You will recognize multiple opportunities for action; opportunities that have always existed but were imperceptible to you before you began to view yourself as a positive leader.

How great the impact and how grand the changes you can facilitate—how far-reaching your leadership can be—is limited by your talents and abilities but these boundaries are not nearly as confining as you imagine. It is like sitting in the middle of an unknown body of water where you see nothing but water on the horizon, in any direction. You do not know whether you are in Lake Erie or the Pacific Ocean and until you strike out, using all of your talents and abilities, you will never know the answer to such questions.

Your leadership potential is also limited by other factors. Things like commitment, dedication, courage, faith, work ethic, persistence, etc., and these are things over which you have enormous control. The number of human beings in the world today who extend themselves to the full limit of their talents and abilities would probably not fill a large arena. For the overwhelming majority of us, the things that constrain us are things that we control, whether we know it or not.

Being an action leader means you are willing to pay the price for success. It means a willingness to work long hours, make personal sacrifices, delay material gratification, and forego leisure and social activities. Whatever it takes, you are willing to give. This takes real courage because, in our society, inordinate value is placed on working as few hours as possible; on reaching a point where sacrifices are unnecessary; where material wealth is abundant; and, where leisure time is paramount. To give these things up for a goal or objective no one else can see is an act of heroism and the world needs all the heroes it can get.

Most people want good things for themselves and their families but few are willing to work hard to get them. They are unwilling to pay the price. It is a tragedy! The joy of accomplishing things, of reaching for something and achieving it, far exceeds the joy that can be experienced from a television screen or from other leisure time activities.

**Inertia**

For most people, overcoming inertia is a challenge. Inertia is a powerful force, or so it appears, that impedes the progress of change. How do we define inertia in this example? It is the difficulty we face in taking the first step, in changing any part of our life. It is the resistance we feel when we need to get up from our easy chair to start a project, when part of us wants only to be entertained.

How powerful is inertia? Try pushing a stalled car. A huge effort is required to get the thing rolling but once it has started to move, less effort is required to sustain that movement. The energy of the object is directed toward preserving the status quo. Once that status is disturbed, the energy can be channeled into the mission.

The effort required of human beings to bring about a change in their lives is equally great, at first, but once the first step is taken the energy that was present, seemingly dormant, can be harnessed for productive work. Some individuals never overcome the inertia that holds them in check—they describe themselves as being devoid of energy. The longer they remain locked in this pattern of minimal activity the more powerful the inertial force appears. Once one breaks free, however, and develops a pattern of directed action, one discovers an ever-increasing source of energy; energy that enables one to accomplish goals that previously seemed insurmountable, if even imaginable.

For over seventeen years of my adult life I was addicted to nicotine. I smoked both cigarettes and a pipe. Many times during this period I tried to break the habit and just as many times I failed. The power of the physical and psychological addiction that held me prisoner—the inertia—proved too great an obstacle and each attempt failed. Finally, after countless attempts, I succeeded. What distinguished that one successful attempt from all of the previous tries? The difference was commitment. Something happened that convinced me, at the gut level, that I must quit; leaving not the slightest doubt in my mind that I must change this part of my life. In my case, it was the belief that my health was in grave jeopardy. I had suffered another winter season with upper respiratory problems that culminated in a serious cough. After what seemed like days of constant coughing, I began to bring up small amounts of blood. The compelling fear I experienced proved stronger than the inertia that had, for so long, held me in its grasp. I quit cold turkey.

The remarkable thing about the experience was that it was not nearly as difficult as I had imagined. Certainly there were rough days and many packs of cigarettes were purchased and cigarettes lit, only to be crushed and discarded before I was in full command of my addiction. As challenging as those occasions were, however, the outcome was never in doubt.

The same is true in story after story of men and women who have turned their lives around. Some succeed of their own volition and some require help from others but the common theme is the same in each and every case. These individuals reached a momentous point in their lives—they reached a turning point. Whether sparked by some external or internal event, the impact was always the same. Individuals who experience such an epiphany come to a stunning and incontrovertible realization that something has to change, and change drastically, if they are to live.

The death these individuals faced may have been physical or it may have been spiritual or emotional. In any case, the undesirable outcome they envisioned was deemed unacceptable and they were compelled to do whatever was necessary to bring about change. This sudden commitment to action prompted a burst of energy sufficient to overcome their paralyzing inertia. In that moment of breakthrough came the grand realization that the true power of their bondage lay in their mind and not in the external, physical world. The power that had seemed so impregnable, so overwhelming, had been blown out of proportion by their fears and by their imaginations.

It is a simple yet vital truth that few forces in the world can withstand the power of a committed, motivated man or woman. All of us have this power. It is there for us whenever we need it and whenever we choose to harness it. Once we succeed at breaking out of our bondage, we see it so clearly. We realize that we have been trapped in illusory cages of the mind; that the only thing that keeps us from fulfilling our dreams is this thing called inertia. As the comic strip character Pogo once said,

> "we has seen the enemy and he is us!"[2]

Most astonishing is the realization that this power is ours for the taking. It exists for you, but first you must master its secrets. As we teach ourselves to use this power, with increasing efficacy we begin to see the world changing before our eyes. How does the world change? It does not; our perception changes. In terms of making things happen our perception is the reality. It is a story as ancient as mankind.

For generations, the most intelligent people alive believed the world to be flat. The reality of a spherical world had no meaning for men and women of this period; their perception was the reality. Their perception also limited the potential of their imagination just as our perceptions are limited. We are constrained by the inertia that enslaves us and that clouds our vision, thus obscuring the brilliant horizons that are the possibilities in each of our lives.

## Solutions

As overwhelming as many of society's problems seem, there are few that lack solutions if only we will accept responsibility for them. It is only when millions of men and women abdicate responsibility that problems acquire the characteristics that make them seem insurmountable.

---

[2] Kelly, Walt, *Pogo*, Syndicated Comic Strip.

Many Americans have become isolationists in the sense that they choose to insulate themselves from their community's problems. They move to suburbs, resist taxation and annexation; distance themselves from the problems of the poor and the non-white. They do not wish to be burdened by such concerns and choose, rather, to abdicate responsibility to someone else—anyone else. "Just let me do my job, and live my life, and raise my family." "Let the other guy take care of him or herself." "It's not my concern!"

It is this very tendency, to shirk responsibility for the problems that engulf us that is at the root of our problems as a society. Responsibility for leadership in the world is not a burden that rests on the shoulders of a select and elite few; it is a burden that must be borne by every man and woman. Each of us has a clear responsibility to lead within the context of our little portion of the world and within the constraints of our unique talents and abilities. I challenge you to believe you can make a difference; a real difference!

If you are like most people, you are using only a fraction of your abilities and your capacity for energy is under-utilized. You can have better relationships, a better marriage, a more successful career, and the job opportunity about which you have dreamed may well exist right where you are, right now. You can influence the quality of your children's education and you can help your community solve its problems. All of the power required to accomplish these things is in your possession.

I am not suggesting that you can do it all by yourself, but then leadership does not exist in isolation. When you provide positive leadership in areas of concern to other people, you will find them ready and willing, not just to follow, but to share your vision and join in your mission. You may not yet believe that you possess the leadership ability to make this happen, but have it you do and it has always been in your possession. It is only a false sense of modesty that keeps most of us from displaying our full potential.

One of my childhood heroes was Baseball Hall of Fame pitcher and broadcaster, Dizzy Dean. Dizzy was famous for generously sharing his high opinion of his prodigious talents with anyone who would listen. On one Saturday, during the "Game of the Week" Ole Diz was telling the audience about how he used to overpower the opposition with his "country fastball," when fellow broadcaster and partner, Buddy Blattner, remarked with obvious sarcasm:

"Diz, your modesty overwhelms me!"

"Well, pardner," Ole Diz responded, oblivious to the sarcasm, "I've got a lot to be modest about."

In the area of positive leadership, we could use a little less modesty and a little more of Dizzy Dean's panache. Too simple to be true? The message is true—it just isn't as simple as it appears.

We begin with simple concepts because the idea itself is fundamental. It is the rich variety of issues crying out for leadership that suggests complexity. The idea of leadership exists in the context of the human personality and the human organization and it is within this context that the discussion must occur. We will talk a great deal about leadership in the context of human organizations but the principles of positive leadership are applicable in any venue and translate to any situation or circumstance.

**Preliminary Definitions**

Webster's Dictionary defines the verb "lead" as "to go first," and "to show the way." The word suggests both the initiation of action and a grasp of its purpose. Implicit is acceptance of responsibility for making something happen. Virtually every human action has an object; it may be conscious or subconscious, voluntary or involuntary, but each action is purposeful. The concepts of action and purpose are crucial to our understanding of leadership. Effective leaders possess a special vision that propels them to action.

Leadership occurs at all levels of our society. When we talk about leaders we are prone to think of Presidents and governors, of Popes and bishops, of generals and CEOs. What we overlook is that each of us, in the course of our daily lives, plays the role of leader. The majority of people are inclined to claim that they are not leaders because they do not understand what leadership means. They may not be effective leaders and they may not be the kind of leader whom peers will notice, but all of us have leadership ability and all of us exercise leadership on a daily basis whether we realize it or not.

Some obvious examples are serving as a model for our children, giving directions to a traveler, recommending a restaurant, a book, or a movie to a friend. We exhibit leadership when we are first to say hello to someone we encounter. Each of these actions fits the definition of leadership because each action is purposeful and each action impacts on or influences the actions of other people.

Think for a moment about the influence of the simple act of saying hello to a friend or acquaintance. We know how we feel when our existence is acknowledged by another human being. It evokes good feelings. The warmer and more friendly the acknowledgment the better we feel. Occasionally, the acknowledgment comes at a time when we are emotionally down and it perks us up. It may snap us out of a negative spell or fit of depression and help us make it through a day. Just as we may never share the positive impact of that hello with the friend who offered it, we will rarely know of all of the times when we have had a positive impact on the lives of others.

This ability to influence other human beings through our one-to-one relationships gives us incredible power. How often we utilize it, as with how often we exercise leadership at any level of human relationships, is determined by our vision of the world and our perception of our relative importance in it. We will talk more about the importance of self-worth later. That this leadership activity impacts on other people is a fact of immense importance to our understanding of our ability and power to change the world.

The history of mankind is laden with examples of individuals whose remarkable leadership ability has changed the course of human history. They were men and women who envisioned a world different from that which then existed and, of course, they possessed the special knowledge and dynamic personalities that enabled them to make an impact of such magnitude.

In some instances, the changes initiated by these leaders were massive, involving whole nations or empires and in other instances they were more subtle, affecting the way people thought about the world but which had, nevertheless, significant impact on the society as a whole. Whatever the impact and regardless of the theater in which they played, these historical figures had common characteristics. They possessed an idea new to the world and had the strength of character to act on that idea.

Are these larger-than-life men and women that much different from you and me? The differences, if they exist at all, are one of degree. Although you and I may lack the grasp of physics necessary to develop a theory of relativity or the artistic ability to paint a Mona Lisa, at one time or another many of us have had an idea or fresh way of thinking about the world, which if implemented, would have had a positive, significant impact on our society. Unlike the makers of history, however, we lack the drive to go out into the world to promote our idea. We opt for inaction rather than action.

You and I perceive our ideas as less important. We judge them inadequate next to the ideas of Copernicus, Newton, Galileo, Jefferson, or an Einstein. We also lack the dynamic strength of character possessed by the greats of history, a strength that thrusts their ideas onto the world's consciousness.

This brings us to four of the simple truths that are at the heart of our message. Truths that, if accepted, can alter your life:

1. Regardless of how insignificant our ideas may seem when compared to those of Einstein's theory of relativity, it is a simple truth that the world needs every positive new idea it can get. After all, the differences are relative.
2. The simplest idea, when spoken aloud, will be heard by more people than the unspoken ideas of an Einstein.
3. That Copernicus, Newton, Galileo, Jefferson, and Einstein were human beings just like you and me, and they died just as you and I will surely die. Notwithstanding their enormous contributions, their individual worth as a human being is no greater than yours or mine.
4. Every single human event of historical significance, since the emergence of our species, has one thing in common: its genesis

can be traced to the fertile laboratory that is the imagination of the individual human mind.

**A Definition of Leadership**

Notwithstanding the many levels of leadership, the term "lead" can be given a simple definition. "To lead is to act on an idea." Or, "to accept responsibility for action."

Consider the following example. You come to the realization that litter is a bad thing and you envision just how much cleaner the planet would be if everyone would cooperate to put an end to littering. You have had a vision; an idea that can result in a better world. In this respect, given the nature of the problem and the fact that yours is not even an original idea, you are like millions of other people. You have an idea but you have taken no action. Thus you have exhibited no leadership.

After much soul-searching you decide to make a personal commitment to refrain from littering and you act on this commitment. You have acted. Even though you have acted unilaterally you have exerted leadership because:

- You have initiated a positive action for the purpose of solving a problem,
- You have gone public and are setting an example for others to emulate, and
- Your act made a difference.

The impact of this commitment may seem insignificant in light of the magnitude of the problem but there is a positive and measurable result, i.e. a small reduction in the amount of litter in the world. Beyond this direct impact, each time another person observes you as you deposit litter into a trash receptacle rather than tossing it on the ground, you influence that observer through your leadership example. Granted, the influence is subtle and its impact seemingly negligible but like the individual grain of sand exists and occupies space on a beach, that influence also exists. It is real.

If you convince your family or close friends to share your commitment, the impact of your action is doubled, tripled, or even quadrupled; hence, the level of leadership you have displayed has been proportionately magnified.

Perhaps you go a step farther and make a point of picking up the litter you find. The impact is greater as is the level of leadership and influence on others.

And so it goes. You begin talking to your acquaintances about the problem; then confronting people who litter; speaking to groups; writing letters to the editor; forming anti-litter organizations; lobbying for legislation; or running for public office. The broader the action, the broader the impact and the higher the level of leadership. Each level of leadership has a measurably greater impact on the world. As individuals escalate the level of leadership they exert, commensurate with their skills and abilities, they discover the incredible power that is theirs.

All acts of leadership are important provided they are directed toward the promotion of positive values (the welfare of mankind) and not negative values (the abuse of mankind). The aggregate impact can be phenomenal. Imagine what would happen if, beginning today, each adult American would initiate just one new positive approach to a problem facing our society. The result would be staggering. All Americans, however, cannot act until you act! You are the difference!

**A Starting Point**

Do not worry, yet, about changing the whole world. Start small with real-life issues that concern you where you live or work. Think, for example, about changing your work environment. Take a stand on the issue of productivity or quality and begin to alter the way you conduct yourself and the manner in which you interact with your colleagues. Courage is a prerequisite but such action can impact dramatically on the measurable performance of your work group and on your stature within the organization.

Positive leadership is a powerful tool that can forever improve the quality of your life.

**Leadership: Positive or Negative**

Unfortunately, as with all other human endeavors, leadership can be both positive and negative. In a pure sense, the efficacy of leadership is independent of its social value. Adolph Hitler was a powerfully effective leader who, in pursuit of his warped objectives, nearly conquered the world. He proved just how powerful an effective leader can be in a relatively short time and how dangerous leadership can be in the wrong hands. Fortunately for the world, Hitler was a madman who was ineffectual in some aspects of his leadership activity so that, in the long run, he failed. The counterpoint would be such men as Mahatma Gandhi and the Reverend Martin Luther King. Here were two men who lacked the authority of official government, worked without the might of a military industrial complex, yet changed the world through the exertion of an incredible will and an even more incredible moral courage.

**It Is More Than Going First**

Although we have defined leadership as the act of going first it is a gross misconception to suggest that only the people who go first are leaders. Individuals who go second, third, fourth and so on may also play a vital leadership role within their group. It is rare, in fact, for huge masses of people to follow a leader immediately as he or she strikes out in a bold new direction. In the real world, few individuals elect to subscribe to a new or revolutionary idea right away. What occurs is that the first group of people who elect to take up the cause play a secondary leadership role and influence a proportionately larger group to follow. This process may repeat itself several times until the idea either loses momentum or sweeps the world.

Herd animals offer a simple analogy. The great herds of the African plains contain tens of thousands of animals acting as a group. At the head of the group are a small number of dominant animals and at the head of this small group is a single dominant creature. Visualize the herd's behavior. A lead animal determines, somehow, that the time has come to move on to a new grazing area. This leader has, we might say, an idea and he or she acts on that idea by striking out toward a new food supply. Possibly, in addition to moving out, the leaders communicate to the animals around him or her in some way. In any case, the animals in close proximity to the leader begin to follow. Soon, other animals observe their brethren moving and, as they are bred to do, begin to follow.

The herd is large, however, and at its opposite edge there is, as of yet, no sign of movement and no awareness of a leadership decision. But, gradually, like a chain reaction, more and more of the animals are responding to the leadership of their herd-mates until, finally, the entire herd is on the move. Many of these animals will continue to move long after their leaders have stopped.

The leadership of the dominant animal is conveyed through multiple layers of leadership in such a way that every animal of the herd is influencing the behavior of some other animal. Even the last animal to move, the lowliest beast of them all, plays out the role. It responds like all the rest, no doubt unaware, living as it does in a perpetual cloud of dust, that there is no one left to follow.

Human behavior shares similarities with the herd animals of our example. Through the power of mass communication we may be able to see firsthand that which is happening on the outer edge of the herd, but our behavior is influenced significantly by the leadership of the common folk who reside around us. We may hear a President's call to action but most of us wait to see what our friends and families think before we commit ourselves.

This "rippling" or "snowball effect" is evidenced in most human activity. It creates numerous opportunities for individuals to influence group behavior. We suggest that the role of the individual, because of this "rippling" effect, is far more powerful than is commonly understood.

Further pursuit of our analogy reveals another point. The preservation of the group requires that each animal accept responsibility for its safety. The dominant animals cannot be everywhere and cannot solve all problems. When predators strike at the far edge of the herd every animal shares a responsibility to act. If all waited for the leader to sound an alarm the herd would be easy prey for its enemies and to the dangers of the natural environment. Therefore, whoever first recognizes the danger is expected to lead and the herd will respond regardless of which individual creature acted.

In the world of human organizations, the same responsibilities would appear to exist. Possibly we have become too civilized, however. We see dangers facing the world but seldom are we motivated to leave the apparent security of our homes to act, content instead, to rely on our elected representatives to act on our behalf. This may well account for the dilemma in which we find ourselves as a society; that the common man and woman disclaims responsibility for the preservation of the common good.

This apathy, which seems so pervasive, can be combated if people are shown that they have the power to influence events. Yet, it is not an easy task and the sense of hopelessness appears deeply entrenched. Have we been conditioned to believe we are powerless?

Is this an inevitable risk of a representative form of government, that when we elect someone to represent our interests there is a tendency to think our job is done, our responsibility fulfilled? We abdicate our responsibility and we then allow outside forces to influence our elected representatives. The result is the legislator who is more heavily influenced by lobbyists and political action committees than by his or her constituents.

We return to our premise that not only can individuals make a difference, individuals bear responsibility for the events around us and for the quality of life throughout the world. Each of us possesses the ability to exert positive influence and has a clear and unequivocal responsibility for positive leadership. Whether the individual rises to the highest levels of leadership of his or her nation, state, community, or enterprise is irrelevant. Whatever our designation, the more openly we embrace the leadership role the more success we will enjoy and the greater our contribution to the world.

**Positive Values**

Leadership is taking a stand; speaking out; it is positive action on behalf of a cause or value system. Positive leadership is normative. It is leadership in pursuit of positive values. Those values are rooted in the concepts of peace, justice, freedom, democracy, prosperity, and equal opportunity for all peoples of the Earth. These are the values expressed in the American Constitution and in the Bill of Rights. They leave no room for racism, sexism, or religious persecution. To these we add the values of hard work, honesty, and teamwork.

Positive leadership is concerned with advancing the often forgotten American ideal that society can accommodate people of all cultures. These people must be willing to assimilate to the extent that they agree to participate and to contribute to the economic and political systems, and to the extent that they respect the rights of other groups and other individuals. Beyond that, they are free to preserve and protect their cultural and religious identities.

This "melting pot" concept appears to be an idea fallen in disfavor. Some segments of our society seem more inclined to promote their own culture as the only true American way. In fact, there is no one true American way. It is not conservative Christian, it is not Catholic, and it is not white Anglo-Saxon protestant. The American way is pluralism. Nothing threatens the security of our way of life or is more dangerous to the principles of democracy than the notion that there is only one true America. Nor can we embrace a system that suggests that the American way is only for Americans.

Events across the globe suggest that there is a hunger for freedom and democracy, but there is an important lesson we need to learn. We cannot create democracy by decree or by the mere overthrow of totalitarianism. Events in Russia since the fall of the Soviet Union provide ample evidence. We forget that, in the United States, it took nearly a century to get democracy to work well and we struggle continuously with the demands and challenges of a democratic form of government. Democracy requires an incredible tolerance if it is to work. It is also apparent that we have come to take freedom for granted.

Before we can teach the emerging nations of the world how to make freedom work, we must recapture the magical spirit ourselves. The value systems advanced by positive leaders must embrace all peoples of the planet regardless of their racial group, culture, religion, or level of economic development. And, it requires the effort of every single American. Imagine for just one moment what the world would be like if every person on the globe was a free and committed advocate of 1) the democratic ideal, 2) of the preservation of our environment, and 3) of the sanctity of human life. Imagine what our nation would be like if this were the reality here at home. What a marvelous place it would be. The simple secret of life is that such a world or nation is possible but it cannot happen without you. Do not wait for someone else—go first!

**Leadership on the Job**

The role of leadership is equally important to our economic systems and much of this book is devoted to concepts you can apply on your job, whether you work on a production line, in an office, in sales, or are a member of management and, therefore, part of a formal leadership structure. The success of any business venture is as much a result of its leadership as any other force or influence. The contributions of Tom Peters and his colleagues are of immense importance to our discussion of leadership, an importance that transcends their popularity a decade or more ago.

In *A Passion for Excellence: The Leadership Difference*, Peters and Nancy Austin write:

> . . . the concept of leadership, is crucial to the revolution now under way – so crucial that we believe the words "managing" and "management" should be

discarded. "Management," with its attendant images – cop, referee, devil's advocate, dispassionate analyst, naysayer, pronouncer – connotes controlling and arranging and demeaning and reducing. "Leadership" connotes unleashing energy, building, freeing, and growing."[3]

They concur that leadership is about accepting responsibility and that it must reach throughout the organization and involve all people within the organization. They go on to say:

"In the past two decades the most exercised part of the corporate body has been the pointing finger. If in doubt, blame it on OPEC, the Japanese, EPA, OSHA, EEOC, etc. Some didn't. Some looked to the talent they were given and seized the moment. . . .

So that is our model: care of customers, constant innovation, turned on people. Yet one thing is missing, one element that connects all others. It was a shadow over the pages of *In Search of Excellence*, but was seldom labeled, as many subsequently pointed out. It is leadership. Leadership means vision, cheerleading, enthusiasm, love, trust, verve, passion, obsession, consistency, the use of symbols, paying attention as illustrated by the content of one's calendar, out-and-out drama (and management thereof), creating heroes at all levels, coaching, effectively wandering around, and numerous other things. Leadership must be present at all levels of the organization. It depends on a million little things done with obsession, consistency and care, but all of those

---

[3] Austin, Nancy and Tom Peters, *A Passion For Excellence: The Leadership Difference*, Grand Central Publishing, New York, 1989.

million little things add up to nothing if trust, vision and basic belief are not there."[4]

The trilogy: *In Search of Excellence*[5], *A Passion for Excellence*[6], and *Thriving on Chaos*[7], is a rich source of evidence to support the importance of leadership in the real world of the business enterprise. As with most of the concepts that we discuss, these ideas have great applicability to our family and social lives as well.

## Leadership is About Individual Men and Women

Our purpose in *The Difference is You: Power Through Positive Leadership*, is not to duplicate but to add to the body of knowledge on the subject of leadership. Although we will often discuss leadership in the context of a business organization, our emphasis is always on you as an individual human being and the personal challenges facing you as you embark on a commitment to a life of positive leadership.

How can I make a difference? How do I utilize my potential? How do I get the attention of management? How do I motivate my people? How can I deal with the stress and pressures and still be effective? How can I get more enjoyment out of my life?

These frequently asked questions are among the many answered in *The Difference is You: Power Through Positive Leadership*.

A manager of a minor league baseball team serves as a good illustration of the type of leader we are seeking. His success is directly linked with the success of his players. He can come no closer to reaching his goal of moving up to the major leagues unless many of his players do well and move up, also. If his team members perform poorly, he and they will go nowhere. Therefore, he constantly teaches and

---

[4] Austin and Peters, 1989.
[5] Peters, Thomas J. and Robert H. Waterman, *In Search of Excellence*, Harper and Row, New York, 1982.
[6] Austin and Peters, 1989.
[7] Peters, Tom, *Thriving on Chaos*, Harper Paperbacks, New York, 1990.

strives, through the utilization of his leadership skills, to bring out the optimum development of his players.

Our goal is to get you, the reader, turned on to leadership. Why? Because it's fun, it's exciting—so exciting that it brings sparkle to your whole life—and it allows you to accomplish truly marvelous and astonishing things.

In many respects, leading people is like gardening. If one does not tend to the needs of one's plants, replenish the nutrients in the soil, root out the weeds, and continuously adapt our actions to the changing environment the harvest will be diminished and eventually the soil will be exhausted. On the other hand, the leader who fully tends to these things will have an abundant harvest and long-lasting productivity.

**Leadership Redefined**

Examine, if you will, our subtitle: The Power of Positive Leadership. Five words, three of which are operative. What do you see?

Focus, first, on "Leadership." Leadership is the single-most important characteristic of successful groups or organizations. Since everything men and women do is done in the context of groups or organizations (we are, after all, social animals), leadership is paramount.

What does the word "Positive" contribute? It suggests that we are concerned about values that contribute to making things better, not worse. It is an acknowledgment that values are important; that whatever our values may be they drive, even compel us. We also use "positive" to mean pro-active. It implies a constant forward movement. As we will learn later, positive leaders are action leaders. They make things happen!

Finally, the word "Power." Leadership creates power and the effective utilization of power enables leaders to accomplish goals, to do things—remarkable and extraordinary things. Positive leadership is social electricity; it gives one the power to do good things—the power to make a positive contribution to your group or cause—wherever you are. This power is incredible and it is there for you if only you reach out for it; it is there for anyone who will open his or her heart and mind. It will change your life and it will change the world in the process.

**Leadership Leads to Success**

Leadership is essential to the success of any human endeavor. In business, leadership is a powerful force that propels the enterprise toward fulfillment of its mission. Organizations directed by strong, dynamic leaders—individuals who believe in positive values and who are committed to infusing their organization with those values—will have unparalleled success.

Few businesses begin with a bad idea or with an unmarketable product or service. Yet fail businesses do, in great numbers. Statistics from the Small Business Administration suggest that over sixty percent of new business ventures fail within the first six years of start-up.[8] Nearly as significant as the failures is the number of businesses that survive, but only marginally. Others appear healthy but never truly flourish.

Inevitably, business failure is a consequence of: 1) mismanagement at one or more critical junctures in the process of converting a potentially profitable business concept into an achievable business plan; and, 2) failure to take effective and efficient action (productivity and performance) over a sustained period of time. Many companies prosper, only to falter during transition from small venture to large. These initiatives miss the mark when the demands placed on leadership swell more quickly than the growth in leadership's prowess. Still others stumble in spite of past successes, a consequence of leadership's inability to recognize changes in the business environment and respond appropriately and effectively.

Business men and women take enormous, though calculated risks in order to gain a competitive edge for their company or to significantly enhance their market share. They are imbued with an entrepreneurial spirit that thrusts them toward opportunity wherever they find it. As much as has been learned in this century about

---

8   U.S. Small Business Administration, Office of Advocacy, Small Business Data Base USELM file, version 9, November, 1987.

the importance of management leadership to the ultimate success of the business enterprise, the role of leadership is routinely undervalued and underestimated. It is not surprising, therefore, that these same aggressive risk-takers balk when presented with an opportunity to invest modest resources toward the development of their own leadership skills and those of their executive and middle management staff. They opt, instead, to manage their companies intuitively, trusting their brilliance, their instincts and, yes, their good fortune to see them through.

More conservative managers will take only the most guarded risk, and only when events compel them to choose action over inaction. To these individuals, an investment in the development of leadership personnel seems frivolous and ill advised. These business men and women rely on tradition.

Management is more than a mechanistic process applied to business problems—it has an emotional component. The human relations' school of management was an acknowledgment of this emotional component, but it stopped short of grasping the essence of management. The worker, however remarkable his potential, did not respond with greater productivity simply from being treated well. A key ingredient was missing.

That key is leadership. It takes leadership to make management successful. Managers who create systems to bring out the highest level of performance of their people and then sit back and watch while the system is implemented will often be successful. But, leaders who devise systems to bring out the highest level of performance of their people and then go out among those people and lead them through the process are almost universally successful.

Leaders sell their people on the company's mission. They teach them the values, walk the floor with them when it's necessary, and drag them screaming and hollering into the future when that is necessary. What leaders do not do is sit back and wait for something to happen. Leaders are pro-active. They do all the other things managers do. They plan, organize, set objectives, and establish controls and they do these things well. The distinguishing characteristic of leader-managers, in contrast to people who simply manage, is the commitment to personal involvement and positive action. Leaders make good things happen.

Profitable organizations require leadership that concentrates on developing the strengths of the enterprise; leadership promoting those things that are right about the organization. Examples of negative leadership abound. They include managers who only criticize; people who talk only about problems, not solutions; individuals who concentrate their efforts, not so much on selling their ideas as on denigrating the ideas of others. Positive leaders, in contrast, embrace the credo that one can accomplish far more by building people up than by tearing them down. They are not concerned with assigning blame but with solving problems and learning from mistakes. Positive leaders teach their people to be strong and independent rather than weak and dependent. Ultimately, they strive for interdependence.

Positive leadership is a special kind of leadership that brings out the best of an organization, insures that its objectives are the right ones, that its methods are the best methods, that its resources are cultivated to their optimal level, and that keeps the enterprise moving relentlessly toward fulfillment of its dynamic mission.

## PHILOSOPHICAL FOUNDATIONS

As we embark upon this discussion of Positive Leadership, remember that we are not breaking new ground so much as we are re-examining conventional wisdom; testing some of the basic concepts that have sustained us for generations. Our approach is an eclectic one that contends that the individual human being has a unique ability to direct his or her energies so as to live a positive life and that this same individual has the potential, through positive leadership, to re-fashion the world around him or her.

The thrust of this concept is simple. Individual men and women can make a difference. Regardless of how troubled one's surroundings, no matter how hopeless it may seem; no one is powerless. Each of us can have a positive impact on the people with whom we interact and upon the organizations in which we participate.

**The Four Philosophical Foundations of Positive Leadership**

The theory of Positive Leadership is rooted in four fundamental ideas or principles:

1. <u>The Positive Principle</u>.

The philosophical foundation of our Theory of Positive Leadership begins with the Positive Principle, which was introduced by Norman Vincent Peale in his seminal work, *The Power of Positive Thinking*, first published in 1952. The essence of the Positive Principle is that anything man can imagine, man can do. It is only when one has a belief in the possibility of a thing that it becomes possible.

2. <u>It is Better to Give than to Receive</u>.

The second cornerstone of our Theory of Positive Leadership is constructed on the axiom, "it is better to give than to receive." Everything human beings do is done in the context of organizations. The success of an organization is contingent upon the willingness of individuals to give of themselves for the betterment of the organization. Noted motivational speaker, Zig Ziglar writes:

"You can get everything you want and need out of life if you help enough other people get what they want and need![9]"

The essence of Ziglar's message is: not only is it better to give than receive but the more you give of yourself, the more you receive in return.

---

9   Ziglar, 1982.

3. <u>People are the most important resource of any organization</u>.

The value of all other assets of an organization is measured in terms of their utility to people. Without people organizations do not exist. Everything we do is measured in terms of our relationships with others. Leaders who are genuinely concerned about people act in ways that help human beings feel important. Helping men and women feel important is the most powerful motivational force in the world.

Nothing can be accomplished in life without people. Many managers only use people and are able to move forward only as long as people are willing to be used. Positive leaders ally individuals to their cause, unleashing the vast power of committed masses. In his book, *Management: Tasks, Responsibilities, Practices*, Peter Drucker says:

> "Any organization which fails to develop its people will fail in the long run.... Leaders help their people achieve success."[10]

4. <u>Organizations exist to satisfy customers</u>.

Organizations have no other purpose. In the case of business organizations, they exist to satisfy external customers through the production of goods and services that meet or exceed the expectations of the customer. One of the great myths of business is the belief that businesses exist to make money. While it is true that entrepreneurs make their initial investment in a business opportunity because they hope to get a favorable return, their choice in the kind of business they will form or in which they will invest is determined by their belief that they can produce goods or services that fulfill the needs of a prospective customer and for which that customer will be willing to pay. Being profitable and making money is simply how we measure how well we are meeting our customer's expectations.

---

10   Drucker, Peter F., *Management: Tasks, Responsibilities, Practices*, Harper Row, New York, 1974.

The moment our focus shifts from keeping our customer happy to simply making money and acting in our own best interest is the moment we place customer loyalty at risk.

These core beliefs lay the foundation for positive leadership and drive us to be the best leaders that we can be.

A positive leader will possess the following attributes:

1. A healthy self-esteem;
2. An understanding of organizational dynamics and an intimate knowledge of his or her own organization including its potential, its strengths and its weaknesses;
3. An unqualified commitment to a system of positive values;
4. An understanding of the essence of success which includes a commitment to action;
5. A broad-based understanding of the needs of people in the work place, specifically concerning those things that foster motivation.

In the balance of this book we will examine the philosophical concepts that drive our theory of positive leadership in some detail. We will look at the attributes of positive leaders and help you learn how to adapt them to your life. Finally, we will outline some specific strategies you can put into action in your own lives, whether at work, at home, or in the community that will produce results and will begin the process of bringing about positive changes in your world.

You can make a difference! Believe that you can make a difference and apply the principles of Positive Leadership and your life and the world around you will undergo remarkable positive change. If you get discouraged or feel overwhelmed, step back for a moment and take a breath but no matter what you feel—do not give up. Such emotions are natural and only part of being a normal human being. Just remember that the world needs all the positive leaders it can get. We are all counting on you!

## two

## The Positive Principle

Dr. Norman Vincent Peale's *The Power of Positive Thinking*[11] provides part of the philosophical foundation for this work and it is no coincidence that the subtitle, *Power through Positive Leadership*, has a familiar ring.

The "positive principle" is an affirmation of the power of individual human beings to lead meaningful and productive lives and to utilize the creative power of the universe. As Dr. Peale writes about his work:

> "This book is written to suggest techniques and to give examples which demonstrate that you do not need to be defeated by anything, that you can have peace of mind, improved health, and a never-ceasing flow of energy."[12]

In this section, we will review the essential ideas of the positive principle. As we shall discuss in some detail in a later section, it is necessary that before an individual can be a powerful positive leader, he or she must be a positive-thinking individual. Simply put, only strong people can be strong leaders.

Writing over fifty years ago, Peale suggests that far "too many people are defeated by everyday problems of life," and that this is "quite

---

[11] Peale, Norman Vincent, *The Power of Positive Thinking*, Prentice Hall, Inc, New York, 1954.
[12] Peale, 1954.

unnecessary. People complain about the bad breaks they receive without any sense of how they, as individuals, can control and even determine those breaks."[13] We do not deny that true hardships and tragedies exist in the world. What we do suggest is that individuals can prosper in spite of them.

This idea is truer and more vital today than ever before. Too many people allow themselves to be defeated by the everyday problems of life. Alcohol, for example, is every bit as much of a problem today as it was fifty years ago, possibly more so, as thousands of teenage children have joined the ranks of alcoholics. Unlike fifty years ago, literally hundreds of thousands of people are addicted to a variety of illegal drugs and controlled substances and, more recently, with prescription drugs. Beyond their own addictions, women are giving birth to thousands of babies who enter the world addicted to a drug, never having had the opportunity to say "no" and never knowing what it is like to live a life free from the grip of addiction.

Whole sections of cities in this great nation of ours are spawning generations of young people for whom the American dream does not exist. All some of these young people know is abject poverty, violence, virtual illiteracy, and a hedonistic philosophy in which fending for oneself and taking what one wants in life are the only strategies they know and the only ones that seem effective.

Possibly most tragic of all, thousands of young men and women feel so alienated from and defeated by the world around them that suicide is an all too frequent choice. And, there are literally millions of people in the so-called mainstream of our society who feel so overwhelmed by the problems of the world and so helpless in the face of those problems that they have become virtual isolationists; individuals withdrawn into a world where they need only be concerned with the preservation of their own pleasure and security.

Helplessness breeds hopelessness and hopelessness breed apathy, which in turn, breeds helplessness, in a vicious black hole that threatens to engulf us all.

---

13  Peale, 1954.

Somehow, and very soon, something must change. This change must start with individual human beings; it can begin nowhere else. It must commence with individual men and women who are not helpless and who believe, unfailingly, that they can change themselves and, by doing so, can begin to change the world around them. Hence, the critical importance of the Positive Principle.

**The Positive Principle**

Dr. Peale's books have been read by millions of people, worldwide, over the past half-century and have undoubtedly changed countless lives. Sadly, however, when we live in a world where millions represent only a fraction of a percent of the world's population, millions are not enough. We must urgently spread the message of hope to all people including the poor, the homeless, the illiterate, and the violent.

In this section we want to accomplish two things, 1) to explain the Positive Principle and discuss its importance, and 2) to secularize the message just a little.

The central idea of the Positive Principle is that "you need be defeated only if you are willing to be." A positive approach offers the individual a set of principles that will bring about an incredible revitalization. The Positive Principle can and will give us control over our circumstances, will enhance our relationships with people, and will strengthen both our self-esteem and physical health.

These are not idle claims. The application of the Positive Principle results in the development of a positive attitude, a driving conviction that all things are possible to a believing man or woman, and an acknowledgement that the majority of the obstacles that keep us from achieving our objectives exist only in our minds. The Positive Principle begins with the affirmation, "believe in yourself! Have faith in your abilities." A strong sense of self is essential to a healthy and productive existence. (We will devote an entire chapter to the subject of the importance of self-esteem as an attribute of a positive leader.)

How does one acquire a strong self-concept?  We do so by filling our minds with positive, life-affirming thoughts and with faith in something greater than ourselves.  Dr. Peale's message is clearly a Christian one; he is after all an ordained minister.  Whether the reader is Christian or not, however, the critical concept is that the individual man or woman's self-concept is irrevocably tied to his or her idea about the meaning of life; that our identity is formed, in large part, by our beliefs and by our values.

All of us experience self doubt on some level, however strong our sense of self.  The Positive Principle teaches us that negative thoughts and feelings of insecurity and inadequacy are learned.  Through retraining, individuals can replace these negative thoughts with their positive counterparts.  It works much the same way in which we retrain our bodies to perform a new task.  We learn by repeating the activity until our body learns what we want it to perform.  Training the mind is no different.  The key ingredients are self-discipline and commitment.

We condition ourselves to feel insecure by dwelling on the possible negative consequences of our actions, creating a self-fulfilling prophecy.  When we focus on the prospect of failure we push success to the back of our consciousness and we risk being overcome with fear; defeated before we begin—never giving ourselves a fair chance to achieve.  Dr. Peale writes:

> "Everywhere you encounter people who are inwardly afraid, who shrink from life, who suffer from a deep sense of inadequacy and insecurity, who doubt their own powers. Deep within themselves they mistrust their abilities to meet responsibilities or to grasp opportunities. Always they are beset by the vague and sinister fear that something is not going to be quite right. They do not believe that they have it in them to be what they want to be and so they try to make themselves content with something less than that of which they are capable. Thousands upon thousands go crawling through life on

their hands and knees defeated and afraid. And in most cases such frustration of power is unnecessary."[14]

The responsibility for our success or failure is clearly ours. It is our attitude that makes the difference. Life is full of obstacles and our attitude in the face of these challenges is more important than the obstacle itself. If we view these barriers as insurmountable we allow ourselves to be defeated before we even begin. A positive attitude allows us to imagine success, not failure, and we begin to search for solutions.

What does this mean to you and what can you do when life's obstacles threaten to overwhelm you?

1. Take stock of your assets and concentrate on them—not on the obstacles facing you
2. Affirm the existence of a solution, visualize that solution, and then believe it will actualize itself.

The Positive Principle was spawned from a traditional Christian philosophy that views religion as critical to man's ability to maintain a positive outlook. I suggest to you that the message of the Positive Principle transcends theological boundaries and works as well in a Jewish, Muslim, or other religious framework. What is vital is the existence of a faith that man is part of something greater than himself.

Just as we recognize that man is a social animal, one who feels more secure and more courageous when he has the company of others, so too is man a spiritual animal seeking to understand the creation. When he feels alone in the Universe he is frightened and timid.

People profit from the support of others and aloneness is often a crippling phenomenon. The greater the support we receive the greater our level of confidence and, hence, positive attitude. The greatest feeling of support comes from a sense of being a special part of the universe. Some may perceive it as a close relationship with God, while others view it as being "at one with nature." The same is true

---

14   Peale, 1954.

in organizations. Great feelings come from a sense of being part of something special.

Today, we live in a world that is so vast and complex that men and women may begin to feel isolated and afraid. For some, the world is full of frightening mysteries and this knowledge only seems to magnify their perception of their own insignificance. They respond by becoming selfish, concerned only with tending to themselves, by rejecting the knowledge of the world, and by clinging to outmoded social and religious traditions. The universe is a place of dynamic changes and even the best traditions must evolve within the context of an ever-changing reality.

Is it any wonder that new scientific discoveries are commonly rejected by organized religious groups who perceive that their special relationship with their Creator is somehow threatened? Often, these people lash out at this new knowledge as if in a fight to preserve their faith. Sadly, these individuals fail to see that their response to this knowledge is evidence of their lack of faith rather than an affirmation of that faith. They are blind to the possibility that such knowledge represents a further unveiling of the greatness and grandeur that is the universe and brings man closer to his Creator, however we envision Him.

The secular, modern man may opt to reject the notion of a personal God with whom he has a relationship, but his need for a sense of meaning and of belonging is very real. He may describe it as oneness with nature, as part of the creative force of the universe, as part of the human family or, in some other fashion, but the need for a sense of belonging and purpose is crucial. And, crucial to the Positive Principle is the individual man or woman's faith that they are part of something greater than themselves—something from which they can draw strength. It is a concept important to the Christian community and to the whole human community.

Those who have rejected the concepts of the Positive Principle because it came packaged in the wrappings of Christianity are urged to look again. The Positive Principle has great meaning for people everywhere, regardless of their spiritual heritage.

One particular statement of Dr. Peale's comes close to touching the center of our purpose in this work and clearly provides a cornerstone of the philosophical foundation for the theory of Positive Leadership:

> "What everyone of us wants, more than anything else, is life. Life is vitality; it is energy; it is freedom; it is growth."[15]

Regrettably, our society dwells too long on the differences between people. Differences are important, of course, as we all like to think of ourselves as possessing a unique personality and singular identity. Our differences also create a rich cultural fabric that helps make life interesting. Beyond this, however, the differences between people are largely over-rated and they are insignificant when compared to the similarities.

Genetically, the differences between individuals, even those from different racial groups, are measured in minute fractions of a percent. Why then do the differences seem so important? We all want the same things in life: health and vitality to enjoy life, the freedom to be ourselves and, the ability to grow to our potential. Each of us wants these things—whether an Australian Aborigine, a Caucasian of European descent, a Muslim or a Jew in the Middle East, a Chinese farmer, a native American, a Latin American, or an African-American in central city U.S.—it makes little difference.

Examine the genesis of many of the social and political ills facing the world and inevitably, at or near the core, is the belief that "me and mine" are somehow superior to "you and yours" and that I/we are therefore entitled to more than you. Unquestionably, the political and social stability of the Twenty-first Century will be determined largely by our success in engendering a true respect for all peoples.

An individual with a positive attitude; with confidence in himself; with faith in the Creative Force of the Universe, however conceived and by whatever name; and, who subscribes to a set of positive values

---

[15] Peale, 1954.

that affirm and promote the welfare other human beings can achieve almost anything he or she can imagine.

How do you change your mental attitude?

1. Visualize yourself succeeding. Picture the realization of your goals;
2. Purge your mind of negative thoughts and replace them with positive thoughts and images;
3. Keep real obstacles in perspective and avoid creating obstacles in your mind;
4. Learn from other people but do not mimic them or hold them in awe;
5. Develop a tradition of repeating positive and inspirational messages;
6. Strive to understand your own motivation—seek professional therapy or counseling if needed;
7. Make a true estimate of your own ability, then visualize yourself exceeding that expectation;
8. Develop a healthy self-respect and believe in your powers, talents, and abilities;
9. Have faith in the wonder of the universe and in its creator, however perceived. Believe in the magic of life;
10. Believe that this faith gives you the strength and power that you need to accomplish all of your goals and objectives and that nothing can defeat you or in any way diminish your personal worth.

To a remarkable degree, success in life is the reward of perseverance. Successful people never give up and never stop bouncing back from disappointment and from undesirable or unacceptable outcomes. They seem to have an inexhaustible reserve of energy while less successful people struggle each day to muster the energy they require. People with negative attitudes are prone to energy loss and approach the challenges of daily life with fear and trepidation; they appear listless, apathetic, and emotionally drained.

Energy comes from enthusiasm for life and from the full involvement of the body, mind, and spirit. Think about the occasions in your life when you were passionately excited about something. You experienced no energy drag then, in fact you had more energy than you knew how to apply. Examine your life. What are the things you consider most important? What are things you most earnestly wish to accomplish? Whatever these things are, take them on as a personal cause or mission and establish a set of goals and objectives. Get enthused and involved in something larger than your own life and you will begin to discover a wellspring of energy that can last a lifetime.

Many of us, in spite of our enthusiasm, dissipate what power and energy we possess through worry—through "fuming and fretting." The Positive Principle espouses a total dedication to positive belief and hard work. The attributes of confidence, boundless energy, and total perseverance do not happen by accident. They are derived from a strong work ethic that trains the spirit, the mind, and the body through repetitive work and through positive expectations. The combination of these two attributes, applied to the unique talents of an individual man or woman, forms an irresistible force.

From 1986 through 1989, I had the privilege of watching a truly outstanding high school athlete display his skills. During his four years of high school, this young athlete established a national high school record by winning 177 wrestling matches without defeat and captured four state championship titles. What distinguishes an athlete of this stature from his peers, apart from his exceptional physical and technical skills? On the mat, Lance Ellis demonstrated total faith and confidence in his ability. His moves were executed without the slightest doubt or hesitation. His confidence was derived from relentless preparation. Certainly not all of the moves executed in 177 matches were successful, but few failed because he held back or performed tentatively. He learned a move, practiced it diligently, and then performed it with total confidence and the highest expectations.

William James writes:

> "Our belief at the beginning of a doubtful undertaking is the one thing that insures the successful outcome of your venture."

When you envision a positive outcome, when you expect the best, when you have trained and prepared yourself for action, when you are confident in your abilities, when you are unafraid of failure you are free to give of yourself completely and unequivocally. You are totally focused and all of your energy—your physical, mental, and spiritual energy—is focused on the challenges before you. Is success guaranteed? No, there are no guarantees, but the odds are clearly in your favor. You have placed yourself in a position to achieve, in a position to win.

Athletic competition once again demonstrates our point. Teams and individuals that keep themselves in a position to win, win more often. Any coach will tell you that many more games are lost than won. In any competition, and life and business are competitions, someone always wins but there need not always be a loser.

When you do your absolute best, when you give a full and unrestricted effort, when you take risks and extend yourself to the full limit of your abilities or beyond, you never lose. The outcome may not always be what you hoped but that is not losing. A noble experiment may not work out but that is not losing. The shot may not go in but that is not losing. Someone else may outperform you but that is not losing.

The only time we lose in any of life's competitions is when we do not give our very best, when we hold back, when we back off from opportunities for fear of failure. Typically, when we have given less than our best or have backed off from opportunities is when we have been unable to envision a successful outcome and when we did not think positively.

Having a positive attitude keeps us always in a position to achieve and people who daily employ the Positive Principle are winners. Today, sadly, winners seem to be in the minority when compared to the huge numbers of people who never give themselves an opportunity to experience the thrill of a victorious achievement. This phenomenon, half-hearted commitment, may explain the general malaise that seemed to grip society in America in the 1980s. Have we been reared to think that affluence comes too easily? Do we confuse affluence with success? Have we provided too many artificial highs, available for a price, in lieu of a real and sustaining high that comes from the sense of achievement and accomplishment? Are we too willing to settle for "half-attainment" rather than make the full effort required for "whole attainment?"

For tens, maybe hundreds of millions of Americans, the answer to these questions is "Yes!" The only way we can restore our nation to greatness, and offer greatness to an entire world, is to change. The willingness to change and openness to change are crucial if we want a fuller and happier life. Our egos must be sufficiently strong that we can admit our mistakes and acknowledge our weaknesses. Our need to be "right" must yield to the desire to "do right." The way to be more successful is not to wait for the world to change but to change ones self. We must do things differently.

Remember Zig Ziglar's advice, "If we keep on doin' what we've been doin', we'll keep gettin' what we've been gettin'."[16] What we have been getting, as individuals, and as a society, is nowhere near what we deserve or that of which we are capable. Again we turn to Norman Vincent Peale:

> "So the formula is to know what you want, test it to see if it is a right thing, change yourself in such a manner that it will naturally come to you, and always have faith. . . .
>
> A man who is self-reliant, positive, optimistic, and who undertakes his work with assurance of success magnetizes his condition. He draws to himself the creative powers of the universe. . .

---

16   Ziglar, 1982.

> It is a well-defined and authentic principle that what the mind profoundly expects it tends to receive. . . . Unless you really want something sufficiently to create an atmosphere of positive factors by your dynamic desire, it is likely to elude you. "If with all your heart," that is to say, if with the full complement of your personality, you reach out creatively toward your heart's desires, your reach will not be in vain."[17]

Look around at the people in your life. Observe your spouse, your friends, colleagues and associates, your children and their friends. How many people do you know who are truly willing to work hard, for a long period, to achieve a goal or objective? How many are willing to pay a price for success? How many people do you know who are willing to make sacrifices today for some future goal or benefit? How many are willing to make personal sacrifices for the common good of the community?

Any reader who can name five people for whom they can answer "yes" to these questions is fortunate, indeed. We have become a people unwilling to surmount obstacles; a people held hostage by our apathy and by our willingness to live in a dream world, taking satisfaction vicariously from the illusory world of television. We partake of the thrill and adventure of this make-believe world that comes to us at the touch of a remote control devise, rather than live the adventure first hand. We do not take chances, except on a lottery ticket against astronomical odds, opting instead for the security of a changeless life.

We have good intentions. We want a clean environment, as long as someone else is willing to accept responsibility. We want to solve the solid waste disposal crisis but we cannot be bothered by serious recycling and we certainly do not want a landfill in our part of town. We want the poor and minority children to have a quality education, but not in the same schools as our children, and certainly not at the cost of a tax increase. We want the poor to have access to healthcare for themselves and their families but not if we have to pay for it and not if

---

17  Peale, 1954.

it will limit the amount of care that will be available to us. We want the world to be a better place, but let the other guy change.

Yes, we have good intentions. We make half-hearted attempts to regain control of our lives and feigned gestures on behalf of our principles. We see a world full of obstacles and we quake in their shadow. We are overcome by a sense of helplessness and hopelessness and we back away from challenges and opportunities, consumed by our fear of failure.

How do we deal with obstacles? How do we overcome the feelings of helplessness and hopelessness? The world is so vast and complex, so much larger than the individual. What can one man or woman do in the face of such odds—such obstacles? The answer is relatively simple. Stand up to the obstacles that control you. Examine them for what they really are. More often than not, at least a portion of the obstacle is a fabrication of your imagination, which, upon closer examination, will disappear. When the obstacle is real it can still disappear if we take positive action; if we attack it with the tools we have available to us and with all of the energy we can muster. Erosion seems infinitely slow, its impact often imperceptible to the human eye, yet no mountain can withstand its force. We must do that which is in our power to do!

Do not be afraid of the obstacles you encounter. None are insurmountable. All problems have solutions and all solutions are possible to men and women who believe in the possibilities. It is the simple act of believing in the possibility of a thing that makes it doable.

We each have the power to change our lives and this is where organizational and societal change must commence. We start by changing the way we behave and the way we think. We work to rid our minds of negative thought patterns and replace them with positive patterns of thought. We visualize good things happening. We establish goals and objectives and we visualize their attainment until we believe them possible, until we believe them achievable. We work at it. We commit ourselves to it and initiate the incredibly powerful force of change.

Look around you and everything that man has done in the history of the world began in the mind of one human being who believed in the possibility of an idea and breathed life into it with his or her commitment to action. The human imagination is the most powerful force on Earth when put to work by positive thinkers and positive leaders.

**Secular Message of Hope**

We choose to tread delicately when introducing concepts that may appear to be theological because our mission is not intended to be a religious one. It is not our position that one must be a devout member of this creed or that, but neither is such devotion an impediment. Religious teaching does offer important lessons for us, however, and we seek out wisdom wherever it can be found.

Christianity teaches that the Kingdom of God is within us. This has huge implications for modern man. It suggests that we have the power within us, both individually and corporately, to solve all of our own problems and all of the problems of the world. It also would seem to suggest that we cannot wait for divine intervention. The solutions to the world's woes are the responsibility of mankind.

Power resides with the Creator and, as the Creator resides within us, that power resides within us also. When we place our faith in the Creator, however envisioned, we acknowledge that we are part of something much larger than ourselves. It is this recognition that frees us to use the power we possess. This awareness, that we are part of a larger whole, not an insignificant part but neither the only nor most important part, is crucial.

It is very much like the love between two people. We cannot experience the complete joy of love until we share it with another—until we give it freely and completely and without reservation. It also resembles a chemical reaction. An element exists in nature and has certain properties and a corresponding amount of potential energy, which remains inert while the element stands alone. When the element is joined with other elements in a chemical reaction, only then is the energy released.

The creative potential of the individual human being, the essence of the creative force of the universe, is revealed in direct proportion to that individual's acknowledgement of and commitment to the larger whole and its value system.

Each of us, in our individuality, has unique powers and abilities. For some it is the power to shape the way other men think about the universe; for some it is the power to compose a beautiful melody; and, for others the power to elicit the commitment of others. For many it may only be the power to influence a small number of people to expand their vision of the world. Whatever our unique ability, we each contribute an essential component of the whole. Remember that any job well done adds an element of beauty to the world.

We must also avoid attacks against people who think differently than we do. Our advocacy must be positive not negative; it must be an affirmation of the power of what we believe rather than as an attempt to ridicule or defeat other people. Today, our world is full of the "we versus they" mentality where we pass judgment on others and declare them to be wrong, to be misguided, and to be somehow unequal to us. Sometimes we go so far as to judge them to be evil and to be our enemy. In this complicated world in which we live, we will not be successful in forcing our point of view on others no matter how rich and powerful we may be. If we want to change other people we must show them a better way to live without having to give up their unique beliefs, values, and identity. We need to inspire people to look for that which we share as members of the human family.

**Disequilibrium**

Writing in 1954, Peale tells of the millions of Americans who rely on sleeping pills to fall asleep at night. That the American psyche was so out of balance that people needed help to take advantage of the "natural restorative process" we know as sleep. Now, some forty years later, the number of sleeping pills consumed at night has undoubtedly grown exponentially. More troubling is the pandemic of self-abusers: drug abusers, alcoholics, people with eating disorders of one extreme to the other, smokers, people abusers, suicides, and the general malaise that seems to permeate all strata of our society.

Here we are in the greatest, most affluent society in the history of the world and literally millions of people are suffering from social, spiritual, and economic ills. We are a society out of balance—in a state of disequilibrium. Why? Because, no system, individual, or organization can achieve and maintain equilibrium unless all of its components are allowed to play their role and to utilize their full potential.

We have constructed a society that systematically excludes certain of its members from full participation. Through the generations, this has become a cancer that has spread almost out of control and that weakens our society just as biological cancer weakens the body. We have consigned whole classes of people to life in squalid cities with minimal opportunities to grow and to learn, and to enter the mainstream as a fully contributing participant. Then we shake our heads, appalled that these urban neighborhoods produce millions of young people full of anger and with value systems that threaten our very existence as a society.

We have four crises facing us today, one social, one economic, one environmental, and one spiritual. Our success in defeating these crises will depend on our willingness to work hard and on our faith in ourselves as a people. Man is a social animal whose success and happiness is measured by the quality of our relationships. There are very few things in life that are valued by man in isolation and everything of value is shared in some way with others. The key to our very survival as human beings, living together on this finite ecosphere that we know as the planet Earth, is that we create a universal abundance mentality.

Man, when fully healthy and productive, exists in a state of equilibrium between his physical, emotional, intellectual, and spiritual components. When one part is out of balance the entire personality suffers. There are numerous examples to suggest that modern man is increasingly in a state of disequilibrium. Just look around you.

How we re-establish man's equilibrium is the subject of this book. The change must start with the individual through the development of a positive attitude. From there, it must be shared with the world, starting with the people in our little corner of the world—our organizations—through application of the power of positive leadership.

*three*

## THE GIFT OF SUCCESS

A dozen or more weeks on the best-seller list is testimony that Robert Fulgrum's book *Everything I Need To Know I Learned in Kindergarten,* has real meaning for hundreds of thousands of people. The values we learned as a child, even if long forgotten, were important and meaningful. If we were able, as adults, to re-learn those values and apply them to the execution of our everyday lives we would benefit immensely.

As we look at the society in which we live, it seems that it is these simple values which we were taught as children that are the most neglected today. Values that teach us to share, to be fair, to respect the person and property of other people, cleanliness, common courtesy; aren't these the very things that seem to be missing?

There is another value we were taught as children that is of vital importance to the world. It is one we have heard all our lives: "It is better to give than to receive." It is a message that exists in the back of our minds, but for many it has little if any impact on our behavior. It is a simple little message that is far more important than most of us recognize.

Human beings are social animals. We live in groups of other people, not in isolation. We form partnerships with our mate; we have a family, an extended family, co-workers, a tribe or community, a city or town. We are part of a nation-state. Our relationships with these groups are based upon the principle that our needs can be better provided through the group than if we were alone. If we give up a portion of our independence the benefits offered by the group offer a fair tradeoff.

For the group to work, all members must contribute according to their skills and abilities, according to their roles and responsibilities. The individual must give of him- or her-self. It is a simple theme. "The whole is greater than the sum of its parts." A group of people can accomplish far more, working in concert, than the same number of people working individually. That coordinated work effort with division of labor and responsibility can more successfully assure the survival of the species.

Some species of animals, such as the leopard, are solitary creatures. They join with a partner for just long enough to conceive young and the balance of their lives are spent alone if male and alone with her offspring if female. Leopards are self-sufficient creatures, able to survive through the application of their independent powers and abilities. The more skillful or powerful they are the more successful. The most skilled and the most powerful lead the most affluent existence. Solitary creatures are virtually independent from others of their species and have neither the physical nor the emotional need for companionship or for joint venturing.

Many other species of animals are, to a greater or lesser degree, social creatures. Whether residing in groups of two or two million they require a group to fully partake of life. Companionship with others of their kind serves both the physical, emotional, and the economic health of the creature. The larger the group the more complex the social structure and, in some instances, the more specialized the division of labor. Members of the group are committed, whether knowingly or instinctively, to the social contract and although they may have unique abilities as an individual, their value is measured by their role in and contribution to the group of which they are a part. They give of themselves. Their energy is devoted to the service of the group and they will sacrifice themselves for the group when called upon to do so.

The survival of the species is best served by the survival of the group and the group's survival is more important than the survival of any one individual. Does this imply that the individual is unimportant? Not at all. But the group's importance is paramount because it alone assures the survival and prosperity of a greater number of individuals. When the individual becomes more important than the group, the interests of the many are sacrificed for a few.

Man is, of course, a unique creature and we in the western culture idolize the importance of the individual, recently even to the exclusion of the group. The challenge of a democratic society is to find the delicate balance between individual and group.

Man is a social animal. We have advanced to our current level of achievement because we have developed a sophisticated system of groups and organizations to facilitate the safety and prosperity of increasingly larger numbers of individuals. There may be a few individuals who are able to go off into the wilderness and survive as an individualist but these few are clearly exceptions. For the rest of us, even though we may value some time alone, our survival depends on the success of our organizations.

For pre-modern man this relationship between the individual and his social unit was clear and direct. The group was small and every individual had a distinct and well-defined role, which, in turn, gave him or her an identity. If the individual was unhappy with his or her role, he or she had a limited ability to negotiate his or her place but rarely at the risk of losing one's place in society. The worst fate that could befall the individual was banishment from the group. It was a fate far worse than death. Some individuals did break off from their group to go it alone for a time but their ultimate survival hinged upon their ability to join or form a new group where, again, the role of the individual is clearly defined.

Through recorded history, social organizations have grown exponentially in both size and complexity in order to accommodate the needs of the world's burgeoning population. Many of our contemporaries decry that complexity and it does present us with an increasingly complex set of challenges. One fails to see, however, how a return to simpler organizations of yesteryear can solve the problems of the present or feed and shelter hundreds of millions and sometimes billions of people. The starvation of whole segments of the population in a number of African nations over the last two decades serve as stark testimony to the efficacy of agrarian societies. Whether we like it or not, the techno-industrial society is essential to our survival both now and in the future. Such societies present many new problems for which solutions must be found, but the social organization itself is essential.

Today, we seem immersed in nostalgia for better times and it is not surprising that we would yearn for a time when things were less complicated. What we really yearn for, however, is a time when our values seemed clearer and when, it seemed, everyone knew his or her role.

Society has undergone such dramatic and traumatic, often-violent change, in the last century that our value systems seem obscured and eroded. So too, have individual roles become unclear. Huge numbers of people have become victims of these great shifts; they have become the unneeded and the unwanted. As much as we might want to believe it, the solution is not a return to a simpler time, to yesteryear, because the one thing we cannot do is turn back the clock.

The solution rests with the redefinition of values within the context of the enormous complexity of our society and also a redefinition of responsibilities to insure that all people have a role to play. Not because it is the altruistic thing to do, although altruism lays claim to a powerful moral cause, but because organizations can best do their work of insuring the safety and security of the whole when all of its members are contributing to their full potential. As we look ahead to the Twenty-first Century, the problems that arise in present day American society because of the fact that huge chunks of our population are not full contributors, whatever the reasons, will place modern society in grave jeopardy. We need to consider the very real possibility that our society will break down when the burgeoning population of non-contributors overwhelms those who are asked to carry the load. We are concerned, here, with functional rather than philosophical arguments.

There may have been a time when the welfare of the affluent in the suburbs of America seemed far removed and unrelated to the poor of our urban and rural communities, not to mention the poor of third-world nations across the planet, but those days, if they ever really existed, are gone forever. Every pocket of poverty and illiteracy; every pocket of homelessness and un-productivity on the face of the globe significantly dilutes the quality of life of the other members of the human family. There are simply too many of us, occupying too little space to think that we are anything but one human family.

It may seem a gross over-simplification to suggest that the lost value system has a single genesis, but we see ample evidence to support our hypothesis. We have, it appears, lost sight of our dependence upon one another. We have forgotten the most basic law of social organizations, that the role of the group is to serve the needs of its members and the role of the individual is to serve the group. What we must recognize is that it is vital that individuals become more concerned with giving benefit to the group rather than taking benefit from the group.

We have become a selfish society, one with more takers than givers. I do not recall where I heard the story but its message made a lasting impression on me. It's the story of a desert traveler:

> *A traveler was walking through the desert and had gone many miles without water; his throat was parched. Finally, when he thought he could go no farther, he came upon an oasis. Here he found a well pump with a sign that said:*

> *"Inside the door, below, is a glass of water. Pour the water down the opening of the well to prime the pump and you will have as much of the cold, refreshing, and life-giving water as you can use. Just remember to refill the glass for those who may follow you on this path.*

> *If, instead, you drink the water from the cup, you will enjoy only the benefit this one cup of stale and brackish water can bring. And, those who may have the bad fortune to follow you along this path will surely die of thirst, as you have left them no way to prime the pump.*

*Have faith, my friend, so that you and all that follow may drink from this bountiful well of life.*

We are all like the desert traveler. If everyone takes, the supply of affluence is quickly exhausted. If, on the other hand, everyone becomes a giver, the supply of affluence is inexhaustible and all will receive all that they require, if not all they desire. We will have replaced an entitlement mentality with an abundance mentality.

The axiom, "it is better to give than receive," then, acquires a whole new significance. From the first time man elected to pool his resources with those of others, to the very present, the success of the group has been contingent upon the willingness of the individual members to give of themselves, even if it means foregoing the immediate gratification of their own wants and needs. Similarly, nothing so threatens the group as the existence of a growing body of individuals who choose, first, to serve their own self-interests.

"It is better to give than to receive" is more than just an axiom; it is the prescription for civilization. Certainly, the problems facing the world are many but there are no problems that can withstand the onslaught of a populace fully giving of themselves. Just imagine what would result if every American would reduce his or her consumption of fossil fuels by just ten percent; if each would reduce his or her purchase of non-recyclable, throwaway items by twenty-five percent and would make an effort to recycle those items that can be recycled; if each would stand up for the rights of all men and women in our society regardless of their gender, race, religion, economic circumstance, or sexual preference; if everyone would vote in every election for candidates that support positive values; if everyone would put forth their optimum effort on the job, just think what could be accomplished.

Yet, this willingness to give of one's self seems alien to many people today. We live in a selfish society where giving one's time and energy to one's neighbor or one's government is perceived as both unreasonable and unstylish—certainly as un-cool. Think, for a moment, about the amount of trust and faith one must have in order to pour a glass of water down a hole, however stale and brackish it may have been, when one is dying of thirst. Possibly the selfishness of our time is a symptom of a reality in which men and women no longer trust their fellow man to a sufficient degree and lack faith that people will strive to do the right thing.

It is a rare occurrence when even a third of registered voters exercise their right in an election and probably only fifty percent of the adult population is even registered to vote. This leaves only a small percentage of our adult population who regularly participate in our "participatory" democracy.

In 1990, the evening news reported that there had been an unexpectedly poor response to the 1990 Census. The Census may be the most benevolent request our government makes on its citizens and still people are unwilling or too apathetic to respond. Think about it! You do not have to go anywhere to complete the Census questionnaire, it doesn't cost anything, and it takes only a few minutes, an hour at most. What could be simpler? And, the information facilitates many of the vital services our government provides to its citizens.

Of the people interviewed on the news, one woman responded that she didn't have time to mess with it so she threw her Census forms away. A man responded that the questionnaire was on his desk with a stack of bills and would probably be the last thing to which he would attend, if at all. Yet another individual responded that she resented the personal questions and was not sure she wanted to share that much information with her government.

This self-centered, me-first attitude seems prevalent today to the extent that one wonders what would be the reaction if Congress tried to re-institute the draft. There would be mass hysteria.

For six years, I served as a trial court administrator and was always surprised and disappointed at the responses we received from people who were sent notices for jury duty. Of course there were many citizens who were willing to perform their civic duty but there was a significant minority who were indignant, often rudely so, that they were asked to serve on a jury. "I don't have time!" "It's not my responsibility, let someone else do it!" "I don't want to get involved!" The excuses came fast and furious.

Still further evidence for this dangerous mind-set of our time is that one of the principal issues on the agenda of any political candidate today must be a pledge not to raise taxes. The word "taxes" has become a word that elicits a Pavlovian response from millions of Americans who talk as if all taxes are unfair. Seemingly lost is the acknowledgement that taxes are a necessary, if unpleasant, tool of any form of government including democracy. It doesn't seem to matter how worthy the need; any advocacy of taxation is a sure-fire way to insure the victory of one's opponent.

We are left with a government full of elected officials who are afraid to mention the word, in any context, and with good reason. It is an issue that few people can discuss rationally and calmly. As a result it is difficult to pass changes in the tax laws even when those changes are designed to more fairly distribute the tax burden, so paranoid is the public's response.

What has happened to the American people who, historically, have always been willing to work hard and sacrifice for their country and their way of life? Granted our government has done little to retain our trust over the past few decades but the ultimate responsibility for the efficacy of a democratic government rests with the people. The occasional failure of government should elicit more citizen participation, not more apathy.

The answer, once again, appears to be a pervasive, systemic selfishness. Things have gotten so big and so complex that the individual feels helpless in its wake. People respond by withdrawing from the battle, desiring only to tend to their little plot of ground. It may be an understandable sentiment but it only exacerbates the problem.

Somehow, we need to re-ignite the willingness, the desire on the part of all of our countrymen and women, to get involved, to give of themselves each and every day. It is our responsibility under the "social contract." Speaking about our primate cousins, Robert Ardrey wrote:

> "Society is the primate's best friend. . . . If he is a
> social animal, then he obeys the rules and regulations
> of his society; and his personal inclinations must, on

> occasion, yield to the necessities of his society. In this the animal accepts and subscribes to a kind of primal morality.
>
> The wild animal is not free... he is an animal who depends on social mechanisms for survival, order is imposed on his inclinations by the demands of his society."[18]

However much we like to glorify our individualities—our uniqueness and the importance as individuals—we, too, depend on society for survival. We depend on it for our survival as an individual and for our survival as a species. We, too, are free only to the extent that our society permits. Democratic societies strive to preserve as much individual freedom as is possible and in this we are, indeed, fortunate. If democracies are to succeed, however, they depend on a high level of commitment from their citizens—commitment to giving of one's self. Freedom requires partnership with responsibility.

"It is better to give than receive," is very much a prescription for a democratic society.

By why should we accept this? What is in it for me? Will my life really be better if I give of myself? If I give all of the time will I receive anything? The answer to each of these questions lies in the quote from Zig Ziglar, which we introduced in the first chapter.

> "You can get everything you want and need out of life if you help enough other people get what they want and need."[19]

If you are a giving person, one who strives, everyday, to help the people around you be successful, then you will be perceived as a leader and you will have captured the essence of leadership.

---

18  Ardrey, Robert, The Social Contract, Dell Publishing Co., New York, 1970.
19  Ziglar, 1982.

We are, indeed, a social animal and we live and breathe and die in groups or organizations. Our success in life is measured in terms of the level or degree of involvement in our organizations—by our contributions to those organizations. Leaders guide organizations, maybe from the top or maybe on the fringe but, somehow, leaders guide their organizations. Peter Drucker's admonition bears the same message:

> "Any organization which fails to develop its people will fail in the long run. . . . Leaders help their people achieve success."[20]

How do leaders develop their people? Leaders develop their people by giving freely of themselves.

What do leaders receive in return? When their people succeed their organizations also succeed and the productivity and performance of organizations are the measure a leader's success.

The gift of success is something that anyone can give and it is the essence of leadership. Once you give it, remarkably, you also possess it, in full measure.

Our society is replete with examples of selfishness, of incessant search for immediate gratification. Television, movies, pop music, and video games are so laden with examples that they are a symptom of our time. Many of the heroes to whom our young people look are takers more than givers. They are materialistic and hedonistic. They are rebellious and out to make their point at the expense of society. Some are violent and lash out against their adversaries with total disregard for the lives of people who stand in their way. They have no respect for either individuals or for society as a whole and will take or do damage to the property of others without the slightest hesitation if it serves their own purpose.

Others will steal from their employers or sell items to friends for a fraction of its cost and consider themselves to be cool and are considered so by their friends. Some will get drunk or high, seemingly unable, certainly unwilling, to delay gratification of their wants and

---

[20] Drucker, 1974.

needs. They demand it now! "Give me, give me, give me!" "If you do not give it to me I will take it."

Look around you, it is everywhere; people leading selfish lives and rearing their children to lead selfish lives; taking the easy way out; avoiding tough situations where they may have to take a stand, whether it is demanding that your child behave appropriately or standing up for your values in public.

The world has become a frightening place where it is dangerous to trust strangers; where if you leave something valuable in your parked car, whether locked or not, it will be stolen; where it is not safe to walk the streets at night, offer a ride to a stranger, or leave one's home unlocked. Why is the world so frightening? It is because so many people have become takers who lack respect for other people and their property. "Why should we?" the taker responds. "What have they ever done for me?" Many white middleclass Americans hear these ideas and think immediately of the non-white and the poor. But these engrained characteristics are not the province of minorities or the poor; they are universal traits and where they exist they transcend race and economic status.

These traits and behavior patterns are learned behavior and are the antithesis of an "abundance mentality." They arise out of ignorance, fear, and prejudice and they result in an environment—a society—where we feel unable to trust people who are different from us; where we view others as a threat. We each pass judgment on one another and we draw lines of demarcation to separate ourselves and it is all constructed on the belief that there are insufficient amounts of the things we value and, therefore, not enough for everyone. In such an environment, we cling to and protect the things we value out of fear that they could be taken from us, on the one hand, and we covet the possessions or success of those whom we believe have been more fortunate, on the other. In a world where the chasm between the haves and the have nots continues to grow, the risk of bitter and even violent conflicts increases. Unless we can somehow engineer a fundamental change in the way we think about one another, the portent of cataclysmic conflict moves from the possible to the probable.

We think other people pose a threat to us and, because of our selfishness, indeed they do. We need people to give of themselves unselfishly, not because they expect something in return but because they want to give to their community. We need people who are secure in themselves and who recognize that the way people can feel better about themselves is to give more. Giving need not always be the gift of material things. It may be giving of one's time and energy or of one's talent. It may be doing our absolute best on the job or volunteering for a community project in our spare time rather than watching television and immersing ourselves in leisure activities.

There is nothing wrong with leisure time or participation in recreational activities but, somehow, we have allowed the perceived importance of these things to grow disproportionately to their real value. We all need to play hard as well as work hard and everyone needs recreation and some fun in their lives. We have come to think that we need lots of these things to be happy and that they are our reward for our hard work.

Unfortunately, such things do not bring true fulfillment to people; they only bring the illusion of fulfillment. What people truly need is to feel that they are important and needed by other people and by their community. If each of us would give of our time and energy we would find that it brings us tremendous satisfaction. In fact, if each gainfully employed American adult would reach out to the community and help just one disadvantaged child, there would not be enough disadvantaged children to go around.

Our cities are teeming with lost children. Young people who have no hope, no realistic dreams, no positive role models, no motivation, no self-discipline, no guidance, no boundaries, and no one to whom they can turn who can show them a way out of their hopelessness. These young people are the progeny of adults who have also lost hope and faith in the American Dream. The Dream is no longer real to those men and women and, as a result, it is not something that they teach their children to value or to work hard for.

Look back on your own life. What were the things that enabled you to grow into a healthy, productive citizen? The answer is universally the same. You had someone who gave of him or herself to you. You had someone who cared enough to love you and teach you and say no to you, someone who taught you both by words and deeds. Someone who held out hope for you and who had expectations to which you could rise. Someone whom you knew would be there for you even when you may not have deserved it.

All of these things are still absolutely required by children today if they are to have any hope of becoming healthy, productive adults. All of our nation's children are conceived with the same human spirit, but many are born into a community where traditional moral and cultural values no longer work. They reside in a place where traditional family structure, community, and social values are often so weak that the subculture of the streets—of gangs and drugs and violence—is the only thing that makes sense; the only choices that seem to offer realistic solutions to their real-life dilemmas and challenges.

How can we expect these children to turn their backs on the solutions of the streets; options that, in their eyes, seem socially acceptable and clearly achievable; when the alternatives that we offer seem as alien and as distant as the ends of the Earth? How can we expect these young people to turn their backs on these alternatives when we turn our backs on them?

There was a recent story in the news of a child who was found dead. When authorities pieced together the evidence, it became clear that the child had been a prisoner in his own home. He had been confined for years in a small, dark closet where he had lived a life of desolation and loneliness, of deprivation and rejection. When we hear of stories such as this we are horrified and cry out with renewed vigor against child abuse. Yet, who are we to cast such stones? We, as a society, are condemning millions of children to lives of comparable desolation, deprivation, loneliness, and rejection in the social, economic, and moral wastelands of our nation.

This, also, is a form of child abuse but one that is systemic rather than individualistic. We are rearing countless young people in a violent crucible without the apparent realization that it is inevitable that it is we at whom they must strike out. We are responsible, each and every one of us. As a people, we cannot solve all of the problems in the world. Ultimately, people must take responsibility for solving their own problems. What we can do, as positive leaders, is to relentlessly sell a mission, vision, and values that are centered on giving hope that the American Dream is real and obtainable. And we can also begin to teach people how to take responsibility for their own lives and how to exert control over the outcomes in their lives.

If each of us would give of ourselves fully at everything we do, the world would be a better place. If we would do our jobs! If we would be a better spouse or a better parent; if we would give something back to the community; if we were more interested in finding some positive way to give rather than to expend our energy hoarding leisure time and material possessions, what a different place the world would be.

The world needs givers and lots of them. Be a giver and it will make a difference in the way you feel about yourself and about your life. It will make a difference in the quality of the relationships you have with your spouse, your children, and your friends. It will make a difference in the wholesomeness of your community. It will make a difference in the success of your business or career and, finally, it will make a difference for you financially.

Yes, there is an inherent risk in giving of oneself. What if we give of ourselves and receive nothing in return? What if we are taken for suckers or are otherwise abused? What if we appear foolish or are embarrassed? Nothing worthwhile comes without some risk. But what really is at risk? We cannot lose our dignity by giving of ourselves. Our value as a human being will not be diminished. It is not what we risk but, rather, that which we stand to gain that should motivate us. The prospect is all the joy in the world. Yes there will be disappointments. Some people will let us down and others will even hurt us. These things are inevitable in life and will occur whether we give or take. True success and the most cherished joys in life come, however, only to those who give freely.

If you want a better marriage, give of yourself and be a better spouse. If you want better friends, give of yourself and be a better friend. If you want a more successful career, give of yourself and do a better job. If you want to live in a better community, give of yourself and be a better neighbor.

Giving fully of oneself—holding nothing back—is, very simply, the key to success in life! It is magical, miraculous, simple, and relatively painless.

# PART II - ATTRIBUTES OF POSITIVE LEADERS

Leaders come in all shapes and sizes. They can be male or female, young or old. Talent and intelligence are important but only in determining the scope of leadership one has an opportunity to provide. Of concern to us are the things positive leaders have in common.

Positive leaders consistently possess certain attributes. These are the characteristics that enable them to lead effectively and, most vital to our interests, each of these attributes can be learned. Positive leaders have:

1. A healthy self-esteem
2. An understanding of the dynamics of human organizations and an in depth understanding of their own organization
3. A commitment to mission, vision and values,
4. An understanding of the essence of success, which includes a commitment to action.
5. An understanding of human motivation and an ability to tap the motivation of others

Across the broad spectrum of leadership, regardless of the level of leadership or the size and complexity of the organization, these attributes are constant.

This section is devoted to discussion of these attributes of leadership—these secrets of leadership. Acquire each of these and you can be a positive leader and begin to make a difference in the world around you.

## *four*

## A HEALTHY SELF-ESTEEM

*It is not what you are, it's what you don't become that hurts.*
-Oscar Levant

The first distinguishing characteristic of positive leaders—the first attribute—is a strong and positive self-concept. Positive leaders have a clear sense of who they are and where they are going. They have confidence in themselves and in their talents and abilities. They believe in themselves; they believe themselves to be somehow special. It is this core belief—this strong sense of self—from which the power of positive leadership emanates.

Leadership, as we have already discovered, implies taking risks, forging new concepts, charting new courses, breaking new trails. Leadership means going first—often where no man or woman has gone before. This takes great courage, confidence, and character and these traits, so common to the great leaders of history, are nothing more than manifestations of a strong self-esteem.

Leaders must be outwardly directed. They are concerned about the world and about other people. It is not that their own needs are left unattended—quite the contrary. Leaders are secure in themselves. They know in the deepest part of their souls that they are okay—that nothing that can happen in the external world can diminish their worth as a living, breathing human being; as a child of Creation. From this foundation of a secure ego, they are truly able to give freely of themselves. They have, in fact, discovered that one of the greatest secrets of life is that the best way to serve one's self—to feed a healthy ego—is to serve others. The more we give the greater the gifts we receive.

People in leadership positions with an underdeveloped ego do not yet understand this. They have not reached the crest of the mountain from which they can see the panorama. They spend the greater part of their time and energy advancing their individual interests rather than attending to the needs of their organization and its people. As a result, as leaders they are ineffectual.

In this chapter we will talk about the importance of self-esteem and how self-esteem contributes to leadership. We will look at the development of self-esteem in human beings and finally, we will outline a process that will enable you to strengthen your self-esteem.

**The Importance of Self**

Our sense of self determines how we think about ourselves relative to the world around us and how we think about ourselves with respect to the people with whom we interact. Simply put, if we feel good about who we are we will view the world as a friendly place, full of opportunities and we will view other people as potential friends. If, on the other hand, we live with self-doubt, we will view the world and the people in it from an entirely different vantage point. In the latter scenario, the world will be seen as a frightening place, full of dangers and people will appear unfriendly and intimidating.

It is not hard to see, in this extreme example, how different life would be for the individual with the strong ego compared with his or her counterpart from the opposite end of the continuum. The first, embraces life and all of its opportunities and, daily, experiences the joy of being alive. The latter, shies away from life's opportunities as each is viewed, somehow, as a threat and experiences little joy in life.

In the real world, however, few people exist on the ends of the continuum. Most of us fall somewhere in the middle. In some respects our ego is strong and healthy but there are, as well, aspects of our ego that are not as healthy as we would wish. It is these weaknesses in our self-concept that keep us from reaching our potential.

Few of us fully appreciate the dramatic impact these chinks in our personality create; how much they hold us back, how they crimp our style, our talents and abilities; and, how they constrain our performance. What we appreciate even less is our tendency to be unaware of the role our ego is playing in our lives. We know things do not work out the way we want but we subscribe our disappointing outcomes to external forces.

The performance of two young women interviewing people for a marketing research firm provides a meaningful illustration. The two interviewers were assigned to ask people in certain age groups, who were shopping in a mall, to participate in a marketing survey. The two worked the same area of the mall. Both young women were attractive and well dressed. Both were intelligent, articulate and possessed winning smiles. When observed in the solicitation process, both young ladies appeared to be pleasant and professional. Over the course of the day, however, one of the women was successful in recruiting more than twice the number of prospects as her counterpart.

What she did differently was easy to observe, from an objective vantage point. She approached many more people than her colleague. Why? The answer, we think, is simple. She displayed little or no hesitancy in approaching prospects and appeared to be unaffected by prospects who rejected her approach, who were unfriendly or were otherwise unwilling to participate in the survey. The other solicitor seemed to hesitate before each contact and her body language evidenced varying degrees of distress with each unsuccessful encounter.

So what was different? The most obvious difference was the number of encounters with one solicitor approaching almost twice as many prospects as her counterpart. The second difference was the perceived comfort level of the more successful solicitor. She appeared more focused on the comfort of her prospect while the other young woman seemed more focused on her own feelings.

What would account for these very apparent differences in approach? We suggest it is self-confidence, which is nothing more than a function of self-esteem. The more successful woman evidences no fear of rejection and appeared unaffected by people who were unfriendly or discourteous. Because she was more comfortable, she was friendlier and seemed to smile more readily. The result was a generally more favorable response.

The less successful solicitor was clearly more hesitant and even a brief hesitation resulted in lost opportunities as people walking toward her were often past her before she was ready to approach them.

How does the less productive woman respond when questioned by her employer about her performance when compared with her counterpart? "She's quicker than I am," she responded. "She's luckier." Her poor performance was portrayed as the result of external factors and this is typical of underachievers. Rarely is there an acknowledgement that the performance problems might be the result of internal factors over which the individual has substantial control.

One of the most important points we wish to make is that the majority of the problems we personally experience in the world and in our relationships with other people are the result, not of some mysterious external force but of our own low self-esteem. Ego problems, or more correctly, underdeveloped egos, are the primary influence on our level of achievement. We can all appreciate how much easier it is to place responsibility on someone or something else but such action is both self-defeating and counterproductive. Such thinking becomes habitual and we gradually grow to feel powerless in the face of these mysterious yet seemingly powerful forces that continuously obstruct our path. The weaker our self-esteem the more powerless we feel.

Problems must be understood if they are to be solved. We do not mean to imply that there are no external forces that impact on our lives because such forces certainly exist. The role of these forces in our successes and failures, however, is almost always secondary. The truth is that we control the greater part of our destiny whether or not we know or accept this fact. The ability to control this power, to turn it on or off, is a function of our self-esteem. Once we acknowledge this simple truth, our entire life will be transformed, forever.

Viktor Frankl, in his book *Man's Search for Meaning*, writes of his experiences in Nazi concentration camps. In this horrendous environment, the very survival of camp residents was at the whim of their captors. While many perished, others inexplicably—miraculously—survived. There was little the individual could do to improve his or her chances except to keep their hope and faith alive. Many died because they gave up hope—their will to live destroyed.

Frankl writes that even under these horrific circumstances his life had meaning. He discovered that nothing his captors could do, no matter how terrible or inhumane, could destroy the meaning in his life, hence his worth as a human being. They could kill him or abuse him but they could strip him of neither his dignity nor his faith. The value of his life was a gift of the Creator and it was beyond the reach of others. Frankl discovered that with this knowledge came great power. It enabled him to stay strong so that survival was possible.

This tremendous power is nothing more than a healthy self-concept. When we are secure in who we are; when we truly love ourselves; when our life has meaning; our ego is so strong as to be virtually impregnable. No matter what happens to us, no matter what obstacles are placed in our path, regardless of the personal tragedies we experience or suffering we endure, nothing can diminish our individual worth unless we permit it to do so. Frankl writes:

> "Man is **not** fully conditioned and determined; he determines himself whether to give in to conditions or stand up to them. In other words, man is ultimately self-determining."[21]

The very quality of our relationships with other people is a reflection of our self-esteem. If you feel good about your relationship with your spouse, friends, family, and business associates, we can say with some confidence that you have a positive sense of self. If you are unhappy with those relationships the solution lies within. Work on your self-esteem and you will see dramatic improvements in those relationships.

---

21   Frankl, Viktor, *Man's Search for Meaning*, Pocket Books, New York, 1975.

We spoke at great lengths, in an earlier chapter, about the art of giving and the pivotal role giving plays in a full and productive life. The secret of giving—that characteristic that enables an individual to be a giving person—is that he feels he has more than enough and is willing to share that which he possesses. Steven Covey calls this "abundance mentality." One of the true secrets of life is that, whether we know it or not, we each possess enough of everything we need to not only live the complete life but also to share it with others. It is all there! All we have to do is uncover it and nurture it. All we need to do is learn to love ourselves. Once we truly love ourselves we can love others and give freely of ourselves to them.

Loving oneself is just another way of describing a healthy self-esteem. Until we have developed this healthy self-concept we cannot interact unselfishly with people and form effective relationships. And, until we can form quality relationships and interact unselfishly and effectively with people, we cannot be effective leaders. Leadership is constructed upon the rock-solid foundation of a strong ego. Unless the cup is full, we are unlikely to share from it generously and sharing generously of one's self is the secret to both happiness and success.

A leader who does not possess a strong self-concept will spend the majority of his or her time and energy on personal needs rather than the needs of the enterprise and its people. Effective leaders teach their people to be strong and independent rather than weak and dependent. In order to teach independence the leader must be strong him or herself.

The same point can be heard from David Ogilvy:

> "If each of us hires people who are smaller than we are, we shall become a company of dwarfs. But if each of us hires people who are bigger than we are, we shall become a company of giants."[22]

---

22  Ogilvy, David, (edited by Joel Raphaelson), *The Unpublished David Ogilvy: His Secrets of Management, Creativity, and Success – from Private Papers and Public Fulminations*, Sidgwick and Jackson, London, 1988.

It is vital that a leader be able to derive ego satisfaction from the success of his or her people or the leader will be driven to restrict the success of others in order to "get the glory" or "take the credit" for success.

This idea of a secure ego is not examined sufficiently in discussions of leadership. People in leadership positions with low self-esteem stand out, often like bullies on a playground. They are constantly striving to convince their peers, in dramatic ways, just how strong and powerful they are; yet fail to see that the message they convey is a totally different message, one that earns disdain rather than the respect of the crowd. As a result, the crowd withholds its respect for the bully, much to the bully's dismay and frustration. Unable to gain insight into the dynamics of the situation, the bully struts and swaggers and bullies even more, unable to fathom that his own behavior is making it impossible to gain the respect he so desperately seeks.

The same is true on the other side of the continuum with the shy child who always hangs back, too insecure to join the game and so wrapped up in his fear that an invitation to play will never come that he fails to recognize it when it does.

The very same thing happens with leaders in organizations. Ineffective leaders miss the point that their mission is to serve their people rather than be served. And this idea, as illustrated by Zig Ziglar's message that we can get everything we need if we help enough other people, is the absolute essence of leadership.

If he or she is ever to be truly effective, the leader must sit back and take a deep breath, then say to him or herself: "I'm okay! My cup is full. My job, now, is to help other people learn how to be successful. If I do this to the best of my ability, I will get all the recognition, respect, and reward I need through the success of my people, my group, and my organization."

The story is repeated in setting after setting. Organizations with the most intransigent problems are those with people who let their egos get in the way of solving problems. They do not communicate honestly with their colleagues because they do not feel sufficiently secure about themselves or their status with the organization. They do not admit their mistakes because they fear rejection of others and loss of esteem. They see such admissions as a weakness rather than evidence of strength and confidence.

These obstacles are often invisible to the casual observer and, therefore, rarely receive leadership's attention as they strive to tackle the practical manifestations of these maladies. Examples are many:

1. A construction company continues to lose money while field leadership and the estimators argue over blame for company's inability to bring projects in under budget.
2. A distribution company struggles with inefficiencies while inside sales and purchasing battle with data processing over responsibility for an effective management information system.
3. A nursing home's market share dwindles while the assessment team and the social services staff argue about who should control the scheduling of admissions.

How and when are such problems resolved? Only when people are willing to pull down their defensive apparatus and, at least temporarily, place the quest for a solution above ego-protection on their priority list. Only when people learn that it is more important to do right than to be right. Only when they accept responsibility for the problem.

The individuals most willing to place themselves at such risk are those with the most well developed sense of self. Hence, they are the most effective problem-solvers.

Leaders who are most effective at breaking down these barriers between their people are the leaders who pay attention to the egos of their people and who set the right example. Naturally, it is their own strength of character that enables them to take such actions. They are not easily threatened because they know and like themselves. They are focused on the mission of the organization and on their mission as a leader. They spend no time worrying about how the outcome will affect them personally because they are totally confident and totally secure in themselves.

They understand, as Viktor Frankl learned, that what others say, do, or think about them cannot diminish their worth as a human being. Nor can external forces of any kind diminish it. When we feel good about ourselves we can reach out to people and need have no fear of rejection. We understand that not everyone will respond to us in a positive way and, more importantly, that their lack of a positive response to us is a reflection of their own self esteem, not ours. We quickly learn that the more we reach out, the more people will respond with friendship and cooperation.

People with weak egos spend a great deal of energy fretting about what other people are going to think. I recall a conversation with my father in which I asked him, "Aren't you worried about what people are going to think?" He responded, "I prefer to let them worry about what I think."

When we are not worried about our footing we can tackle big challenges with confidence. When we are secure in ourselves we can be outer-directed. We do not have to be concerned with being right all the time or with getting all the credit because we understand that it is the big picture that brings us meaningful recognition. Long-term success requires many ups and downs along the way. We will have our bumps and bruises. They may be painful but they do us no injury.

Even positive people have bad days—days when things seem to go wrong no matter how hard we try but these are accepted as part of the natural rhythm, the ebb and flow of life, and they are taken in stride. Positive people also learn how to take the good times in stride. They do not allow themselves to get too high when things are popping or too low when things are not; otherwise all their energy would be consumed going up and down. Positive leaders utilize their reservoir of energy moving forward. The ups and downs are inconsequential—a natural occurrence in a full life much like scuba divers can expect to get wet and farmers can expect to get dusty.

Accepting difficulties and inconveniences is an important skill, for such things are an inevitable part of living a full and productive life. People who allow themselves to be frustrated by these events suffer unnecessary stress. Once one learns to handle these events in a calm and detached manner one's energy level will remain high and one's ability to enjoy life will increase immensely. For one thing, when you spend little or no time agonizing over inconsequential and insignificant things there is more time to observe and enjoy the beauty of the world and these things are vital if the positive energy level of a dynamic, positive leader is to be sustained.

## THE DEVELOPMENT OF SELF ESTEEM

Man has learned much about the development of the human ego, the sense of self, but there is much more to learn. We acknowledge at the outset that the human mind and human emotions are incredibly complex. They are influenced by genetics and by the physical and emotional environment and the impact of these influences can be both dramatic and magnificently subtle. In the end, they help determine who we are, what we feel, what we think, how we behave and how we interact with other human beings.

It may sound simple but take any individual human being and, short of intensive therapy, it is next to impossible to retrace all of the events and occurrences that have helped shape their personalities and their egos in all of their richness and complexity.

This book is not a scientific treatise on the human personality. We leave that to professionals. We cannot proceed much farther, however, without drawing some conclusions, making some assumptions and inferences that will contribute to our purpose. That purpose is not to identify the etiology of our sense of self but to take what we have at any given point in time and improve upon it, maximize it, reshape it in such a way that it will help us, first, establish worthy goals and objectives and then achieve them.

Everything begins with the "self." A baby comes into this world totally egocentric. As they learn about themselves and the world around them the learning process begins inward and expands outward. The better the baby develops its sensory and motor skills the better his relationships with the physical and social world around him. The healthy child gradually learns that she is not the center of the universe but is still secure in her position in life.

Similarly, the child begins to form a value system and learns that there are boundaries of acceptable social behavior. The more clearly and positively these are learned the more secure the child is and the stronger his or her ego. Values form the foundation upon which all other beliefs and attitudes are based and they provide the benchmarks that help the individual assimilate new information so that the world makes sense. So, too, the discipline the child receives from his parents and other authority figures helps shape his personality and helps make him feel comfortable in social situations.

It is vital, however, that these things are taught in a positive way. When children explore the limits of behavior, which all children are prone to do, it is important that they find those limits and that the limits are clear. Parents who let their children go uncontrolled send their children unprepared into the world because there are clear limits of behavior in society. Individuals who enter society without an appreciation of those limits will continually experience and create problems.

At the other end of the continuum, parents who provide excessive control will rear young people who are rigid and unable to fully enjoy life or who, at the other extreme, become rebellious. For neither group will it be easy to live a full and productive life.

It is paramount that parents teach positive values, values that reflect respect and concern for people and that they provide behavior limits in a positive manner. Children who behave unacceptably must experience the natural consequences of their behavior. Natural consequences are neutral boundaries that are intransigent but which have no impact on self-esteem. The child that touches a hot stove and burns his or her finger experiences a natural consequence. The experience teaches emphatically that this is not an action to repeat but it implies no threat to the child's feelings about him or herself.

All unacceptable behaviors of children, as much as possible, should be handled in this manner by parents and other authority figures. In this, parents must be relentless for the child may not be convinced the first time. The stove offers a good example. If the child touches the stove again and it happens to be cool, the child will not yet be fully convinced of the danger and will undoubtedly touch the stove again and, again, be burned. When the consequences are inconsistent the child will not learn until he or she develops the ability to identify, through means other than touching, whether the stove is hot or cold. This will take time. If, on the other hand, the consequences are consistent—the stove is always hot—the child will learn quickly. Our lessons, values, and discipline must be consistent if we expect a child to learn quickly.

Children whose parents teach them no controls or inadequate controls suffer greatly in life. So, also, do children whose parents teach them in a negative way. Here are several obvious examples:

- "Don't touch that stove, you dummy!"
- "Boy, don't you know any better than to touch a hot stove?"
- "You bad girl! Don't ever touch that stove again.

I am overstating the obvious here but, of course, the child is neither stupid nor bad because they touched the stove. Rather, they simply did not know any better, as this was their first encounter with a stove. But children listen to their parents, whether the parents believe that or not, and they file away that little bit of information and it tarnishes their self-esteem just a little. If a child hears these types of negative messages continuously, he or she will suffer significant loss of esteem and this will have long term adverse consequences with respect to their ability to live a full and productive life. And, sadly, they may totally miss the point that "stoves can be hot and they will burn you if you touch them." Instead of protecting the child by teaching them a simple lesson using non-demeaning but, nevertheless, unyielding natural consequences, we have taught the child to think less of him or herself and have neither protected them nor served their best interests.

Of course, healthy parents do not want to hurt their children but these mothers and fathers do not always understand the ramifications of their actions. Sometimes parents are so caught up in their own emotions that they forget their mission, temporarily, a function of their own lack of self-esteem. Fortunately, children are resilient creatures and unless the negative messages are repeated routinely, the child will not be seriously harmed.

Clearly, the more parents can avoid these negative messages, relying on positive, life affirming messages instead, the healthier our children will be and the stronger their egos. What do we mean by a positive message? Here is just one example:

"If you touch that stove when it is hot, it will burn."

Examine the statement. There is no admonishment, no passing of judgment, no venting of frustration or anger, no idle threats, no empty promises, no emotion whatsoever. It is a simple statement of fact and consequence that teach the child about the external world. The less emotional the content of discipline we administer and the lessons we teach the better. Emotional content that supports the personal worth and esteem of the individual is always a good idea. We neither wish to diminish the child's self esteem nor instill a fear of the external world as both are debilitating actions. Of course, there are times when a child may be in real danger and in these cases the parent's emotional reaction simply reinforces the severity of the threat and demonstrates how much the child is valued.

Children who fail to learn to deal with the real world and its abundance of natural consequences in an objective manner will have increasing difficulty in forming healthy relationships with people. They will view everything and everyone as a negative force to be approached with apprehension rather than as a positive force to be approached with curiosity.

Children relentlessly test their parents and in doing so they are seeking a kind of validation. Do our parents care enough about us to be strong and consistent? Are they providing the safety that comes from clear boundaries on which the child can depend? As parents, we need to remember that everything we do and say to our children is a lesson to which they are paying close attention. When they are begging us to give in and change a "No" to a "Yes", they are doing nothing more than testing our boundaries and our commitment. Sadly, many parents do not understand how important it is that we pass the tests that our children administer.

One of the most important things our parents teach us, and that contributes greatly to a child's self esteem, is how to control the outcomes in our lives in the most positive and effective ways. When we give in to inappropriate demands or when we do not respond well to a fit thrown in the middle of a grocery store, we teach our children the wrong lessons. What they are learning, in those unpleasant situations, are not only inappropriate ways to exert control over their environment but we are teaching them tactics that will fail them as they move further out into society. In other words, we are setting our children up for failure and humiliation.

All of us are imperfect and we all have weaknesses in our ego, in our understanding of our relationship with the real world. These stem from a myriad of negative messages that confused us then and confuse us still into thinking that our worth as an individual is somehow influenced by the external world. The more glaring the weaknesses, the more challenges the child will face as he enters adulthood.

The challenges seem to magnify with time. In a way, they are similar to a golf shot. If the ball is truly struck it will fly true and accurate toward its target. If the ball is struck a little off center, possibly by only a fraction of a millimeter, the degree of error will be magnified by the distance the ball travels. What seems like an insignificant difference in golf swings is all that separates a hacker from a professional.

The child learns from all the stimuli and inputs it receives from the environment. This includes the physical environment, the emotional, and the intellectual. If these environments are healthy we can reasonably expect the child to be healthy.

The healthy child is secure physically; receives the emotional support that continually affirms her value; is taught values that anchor her perception of her role in the world; is allowed to learn intellectually about the world through play and other natural forms of learning; and, develops her social skills as she comes in contact with people, both children and adults. The work ethic is taught both by the example of the parents and by the early experiences of formal education. That some children learn these things more quickly than others is inevitable. Positive parenting recognizes these differences in learning skills and applies more patience and attention to those who learn more slowly. These parents understand that pressure on the child, or lack of patience, will not expedite learning but will certainly damage self-esteem.

Everything that happens to us, every experience along the way, contributes to how we think about ourselves and how we think about ourselves is who we are! From early childhood to late teens, our personality and sense of self have been largely determined by the way we were taught to respond to external forces. By the time we have reached our late teens our ego has pretty much been determined for us; others have written the script. As we approach adulthood, we carry all the subtle, negative messages we received while growing up and they weigh us down like excess baggage. We are still influenced by other people in our lives but they no longer have total control over the ongoing development of our ego systems. As mature adults, our self-concept is well developed. If it is strong we will interact successfully with the world and its people and that ego will continue to grow and strengthen with us, continually reinforced by our life experiences. At this stage it would take some fairly dramatic events to damage a healthy self esteem as it rests on a solid foundation.

It might help to think of self-esteem as one's sense that we have a level of control over the outcomes in our lives. Our self esteem and our ability to control the outcomes in our lives in a positive way are one in the same thing. In fact, everything our parents teach us prepares us to control the outcomes in our lives within the context of a system of values. The more skills we are able to apply to effect outcomes and the more positive our values and relationships with other people the happier and more productive we will be in dealing with the never-ending stream of challenges that life will bring to bear.

Individuals with a weak emotional foundation, however, will not fare as well. For them, life is frightening and intimidating and they feel helpless and powerless to affect the outcomes in their lives. Every obstacle seems insurmountable and reinforces the individual's poor self-esteem, particularly as one observes his contemporaries easily overcoming what, to him, seems an impregnable barrier.

Why are we so concerned with this? Because we are concerned with helping people develop their leadership potential, a prerequisite of which is a healthy sense of self. Even though our ego has been formed, the job is not complete. When we reach adulthood, the responsibility for control over our ego-development has passed to us! We now possess the ability, the power, to change that which has been written. It is this very point that is the purpose of this book—that wherever we are, no matter how tattered our ego, we can begin to bring about positive change that will steadily improve our ability to control or influence the outcomes in our lives.

Everything we think and feel and, as a result, the way we behave, is a function of what we have learned. While there is little we can do about external factors that impact our lives or about the genetic potential with which we were born, there is much we can do about the learned behavior that guides our daily activity. Theoretically, that which has been learned can be relearned or unlearned. Some behaviors and attitudes are clearly more difficult to remediate than others are, but all can be remedied. Modern learning theory, studying the way the human brain works, suggests that it is easier to learn new behaviors than it is to unlearn existing behaviors.

Whenever the learning has resulted in a figurative chink in our self-concept, we need to learn new behavior that strengthens rather than weakens. This is difficult enough but what truly challenges us is that we are rarely aware of the existence of these chinks because it is so easy to rationalize them. When we scrutinize our behavior—when we introspect—which all of us do, we tend to reject internal factors or, at the other extreme, we find fault with ourselves. Rather than spur us to action, however, our self-criticisms may destroy or, perhaps, erode our confidence and sap our energy. One of the most difficult things any of us must do is to admit that we are the cause of our own problems. And, as difficult as the act of admission may be it pales in comparison to the difficulty in taking action.

Is taking action really that difficult? Of course not, but many people see their own weaknesses as confirmation that they are not a good person, of our ineptitude, and of our personal failures. In truth, all it really confirms is our humanity.

Men and women with a strong, healthy ego also introspect and also find fault with themselves and with their performance. These findings result in no indictment to the healthy ego, however, but are welcomed as an opportunity to bring about positive change. Once we have made the admission that we are less than perfect it is not nearly as painful as we had imagined. We also, then, see that it is remarkably easy to begin the process of change.

It may help to think of our personality as the surface of a car. A little wax and a little work can make it shine. No matter how hard we work, however, an occasional blemish will appear. Those of us with an inadequate sense of self will get discouraged and will fret over our blemishes. If we are not careful, our discouragement turns into resignation and then other blemishes appear until our once shiny ego has become tarnished and unattractive. Individuals with healthy egos will respond much differently. These men and women will search diligently for blemishes, almost welcoming them as a new opportunity to polish, for it is the achievement as much as the shine of the car that is our source of pride and which sustains us.

A large percentage of the problems we experience or observe each day are the result of low self-esteem. Some people go through life with a chip on their shoulder and see only problems in the world. When confronted with a work of art or a thing of beauty they poke at it and search for flaws. They are bitter and resentful of life and the world around them and they are jealous of other people's happiness and success. These are symptoms of an unhealthy ego. And, there are many other manifestations of esteem problems that diminish the quality of relationships people are able to form. These individuals get so wrapped up in themselves that they become insensitive to the needs of other people. We have all met them. They are never interested in what we have to say but must always top our experiences, if they give us a chance to share at all. Like all of us, they strive for the esteem of others but fail to realize that their behavior is self-defeating and counterproductive.

These people must always be the center of attention, even to the extent of taking credit for the accomplishments of others. In doing so, they unknowingly erect barriers between themselves and the people they wish to impress.

An experience at a baseball game offers a telling example. In a close game of real significance to both teams a young player who had struggled with his hitting for most of the season responded with two homeruns and, in the process, kept his team in contention to win the game. In the newspaper the next morning the high school coach was quoted as saying, "I talked to him before both at bats and we made a few adjustments."

Even if this were true, it is a sad example of a coach who has forgotten his role and attempts to claim part of the credit for a youngster's very individual accomplishment. The coach may well have helped the young man but this is, after all, what coaches are supposed to do. This is their mission; it is their job.

What did the coach accomplish by his statement? Did he display himself as a wonderful coach? Of course not. In fact the incident was interpreted by the players as a typical attempt at grabbing the spotlight and only reinforced the general feeling that the coach had an ego problem and was more interested in his own reputation than with the welfare of his players.

The coach, meanwhile, seemed so wrapped up in himself and his apparent need for attention that he was oblivious to the impact of his own behavior. He had lost sight of his mission, which was to help his players succeed through their individual and team efforts. And, he forgot the most important point of all—that coaches earn respect through the performance of their teams and the demeanor of their players, not through their boasts.

Again and again, the scenario is played out where outwardly normal and intelligent people, often with the talent to achieve great things, unknowingly subvert their own desires because their compelling need for attention and acceptance (esteem) influences them to behave inappropriately. The result is a loss of esteem rather than a gain. And, instead of being accepted and respected, people withhold their praise, acceptance, and respect and they draw back, much to the bewilderment of the individual.

So much of who we are is defined by our relationships with other people—by the quality of those relationships and our ability to form those relationships. We are truly social animals and how well we are accepted and esteemed by the group determines much about how we think about ourselves, about our self-esteem. At the same time, esteem begins from within and it is there, in the privacy of our minds, that we can begin to reshape this sense of self. But we cannot reshape our ego in isolation; we require a laboratory in which we can test our progress. That laboratory is our relationships with those who are most important to us.

Relationships are complicated, of course, and so much of what we think and feel is based upon perceptions and assumptions; our assumptions about and perception of other people's assumptions and perceptions about us. Our perceptions and assumptions are colored and filtered by our personalities so that, if we have a healthy sense of self, our perceptions are more in tune with reality. If, on the other hand, our ego is slightly out of kilter, our perceptions will also be distorted and our assumptions faulty, much in the same way that a poorly focused lens will distort the image it projects.

Because it is so difficult to get inside your feelings accurately, and even more difficult to directly adjust the focus of our personality we must find indirect ways to impact. One of the things over which we have some control is our relationships with other people. If we are able to improve the quality of those relationships it will help our self-esteem grow significantly.

This is a difficult thing to do, however, and it is not without risk because few things hurt more than feelings of rejection or being left out of the group to which we wish to belong. As difficult as it is, however, there are things we can do that will make a difference if we have the courage to work at them and the persistence to hang in there when things get rough.

Why is it that some people walk into a room and everyone notices them and gravitates toward them while others enter unnoticed, almost as if they were invisible? There is no simple answer to this question and there is no one thing that distinguishes one from the other. There are, however, a number of factors that seem to influence this thing we call popularity. Here is a partial list. You may want to add your own thoughts and ideas and they are every bit as valid as mine. The list is open-ended:

Physical Appearance
- Size and shape
- Handsome or pretty
- Mode of dress
- Smile

Personality
- Friendly
- Outgoing
- Ability to talk to anyone (communication skills)
- Ability to listen to people
- Good sense of humor and the ability to smile and laugh easily
- Self-confidence
- Poise
- Courtesy
- Social graces and etiquette (they do the little things such as look you in the eye, firm handshake, etc.)
- Generosity
- Talents (They may possess special skills that place them in the spotlight: good athlete, good dancer, and top performer, etc.

As we examine the list, we see that some of the things that contribute to positive, healthy social and interpersonal relationships or popularity, as we often like to call it, are gifts of birth but many are not. Many are learned behaviors, skills that have been developed over many years.

If we are not born with gifts that tend to bring us instant popularity, then we must work to develop the skills that will help us deal more successfully with people, which, in turn, will help us feel better about ourselves, which, by the way, will help us deal more effectively with people. It is a positive, self-reinforcing, perpetual carousel and we want and need to get on it, now! To do so, however, we must be patient. It takes much work and effort to get it started. The goal will not be achieved overnight and it will not be easy. If we are going to give up at the first sign of difficulty, then we might as well save ourselves the trouble because half-hearted efforts are rarely sufficient. The process requires a real commitment. Most people want to be more liked and esteemed by their peers but not many want it badly enough to pay the price—to make the commitment to change.

Once the cycle begins it will gather momentum, oh so gradually at first, but at a steadily increasing pace. Inertia will come into play and inertia in all forms is a formidable adversary. Once positive inertia works in our favor, however, it can be an extremely powerful ally.

The challenge is this: whatever your age, it took your whole life to get where you are at this moment. You must be prepared to spend a sufficient amount of time to get where you want to be. Whether it will really take that long is not the issue. The point is that it is an ongoing effort that you must be fully prepared to make for the balance of your life if you truly want things to be different. Is it worth the price? The answer is an easy and resounding "Yes!" Will it really make a difference? Does it really and truly work? Again the answer is "Yes!" and "Yes" again.

The biggest difficulty people have in approaching this kind of monumental change in their lives is just that—in the approach. It requires an admission that you are doing things that are counterproductive. It does not sound difficult when we speak the words but, for many people, admitting we are wrong is one of the most difficult things to do. Such acknowledgements may be viewed as a failure for which individuals must be willing to accept responsibility. Those who feel threatened by such an acknowledgement, or in any way diminished by it, often take the easy path and opt for an avoidance strategy.

If you are struggling with this dilemma I urge you to listen very carefully. There is nothing wrong with you. You are one of God's creatures and your life has great value, great meaning, and a great purpose. That throughout your life, you have been taught social, interpersonal and communications skills and behaviors incorrectly, is not your fault. It is not necessarily anyone's fault. More importantly, we are not concerned with finding fault. Who is at fault is totally irrelevant to our purpose. Finding fault and fixing blame are totally negative, unproductive activities and are a complete waste of our precious time. This is true now; it is true at home and also in the workplace.

We need to be concerned only with acceptance of responsibility for changing—for learning new social and interpersonal skills that will help us deal more effectively with people and form better and more meaningful interpersonal relationships. One of our objectives will be a discovery of the unintentional and unconscious things we do that push people away from us and then replacing these behaviors and responses with new approaches that will eventually draw people to us.

Let us start by thinking of a room full of strangers. No one knows anyone. Before any two people can come together and get to know and, hopefully, like one another they must each overcome two barriers. First they must overcome their own fear of meeting someone new and all of the incumbent emotions that typically accompany the fear of being rejected. They must also overcome the unconscious "don't approach me" signals that, often, are broadcast by the other.

If you cannot overcome your own fear you will never approach someone and you will not bring down the barriers that have been erected to keep strangers from approaching you. Even if you overcome your fear but the other person is still hiding behind his or her barriers, it is difficult to make contact.

What occurs, then, in that room full of strangers, is that the people with the least amount of fear and with the least formidable barriers reach out and approach one another. The rest stand alone in the midst of the crowd. How do people meet one another? Through various forms of communication including eye contact, body language, smiles, common courtesy, social chitchat, and leadership.

If you look around the room and make eye contact with someone, then you have made a connection. If you make a connection with them and one or both of you smile, then the connection is strengthened and the door is opened for one or the other to take the lead (leadership) and to speak, to shake hands, to introduce themselves. At any point in this process, the evolving contact can be terminated if one or the other does or says something inappropriate or that is perceived as a "stay away from me" signal.

If the eye contact is broken off or if a smile is not returned, or if the person turns away or seems distracted or even if he just gives the impression of being uncomfortable, the other may well turn aside and seek out someone else. The message that has been transmitted was interpreted as "stay away from me," so the other stays away. More often than not, however, "stay away from me" was not the intended message at all; instead the individual was praying that you, or anyone, would approach them.

What went wrong? Probably a combination of things went awry. The person was overcome with fear; they panicked, lost their confidence or resolve or, very possibly none of these things. In fact the person may have been very receptive in their thoughts to the forthcoming contact but their body language simply sent the wrong message without any conscious awareness that they did so.

What does this mean to you? Is the absence of contact a form of rejection? The answer is clearly no! It means none of these things and when these things happen, do not let them force you back into a shell, to withdraw or back off. These events mean nothing in terms of your worth and value as a person or in terms of the quality of your personality. We all must learn the same lessons, lessons that are essential to all sales professionals. The number of successful sales transactions is as much a function of the number of sales calls, as it is a function of your skills as a salesperson. An unfruitful call is nothing more than an unfruitful call. It is not a failure, it is not a rejection, and it does not diminish, in any way, your worth as a human being. It is not an indictment of your personality.

The same is true in reaching out socially to people. The number of contacts you make is purely a function of the number of times you reach out to people and of your skills in doing so. The more times you reach out, the more opportunities you will have to practice your social skills. If you want to demonstrate leadership, approach someone in a room full of strangers who looks frightened and alone.

A strong, positive self-concept is the most powerful thing in the world. It is a tool that can do any job the mind can imagine. Look at all the great men and women in the history of the world and the one unique thing they have in common, other than their humanity, is a strong sense of who they are. They each believed in themselves and possessed a stalwart faith in their purpose and mission.

The energy that flows from a healthy self esteem and a positive attitude is incredible and will make the difference in your life. The key to making things happen is the ability to focus one's energy toward a specific purpose rather than allowing it to be dispersed on generalities or irrelevancies. How much power does it take to bring about change in the world? It takes all that you possess. Each of us, however, possesses a sufficient supply to literally change the world if only we would fully utilize it.

Power is energy and energy comes from self. A strong, healthy self esteem is like a perpetual motion machine; once initiated it sustains itself. A healthy ego draws on its strength and confidence—and its faith in that confidence and strength—not unlike the magical "Force" of the Star Wars movies. If we learn how to use this force—and everyone possesses it—we will have all the energy and all of the power we need to face all of our challenges and to achieve all of our dreams.

But mastery of the "Force" does not come easily. It takes dedication, commitment, persistence, discipline, and hard work—magically the same things it takes to succeed in any venture. But the truly exciting thing about the concept is that we all possess this power, this force. It lies within us, albeit in unequal quantities.

**IMPROVING YOUR SELF CONCEPT**

We have established that a strong and vibrant sense of self is an essential component of fully contributing members of society and that, for leaders, it is indispensable. But saying that means little if you happen to be burdened with an underdeveloped ego. This section will show how you can strengthen your self-esteem.

Improving your self-esteem is no different than improving any other aspect of your life. If you are not happy with your life, change the way you live, the way you think, feel, and act. Examine every aspect and begin doing things differently. Remember Zig Ziglar's admonition, "*If you keep doin' what you've been doin', you'll keep gettin' what you've been gettin'.*"[23]

Our personality or ego structure manifests itself through our feelings, thoughts, and behavior. Our feelings, thoughts, and behavior are interconnected and it is helpful to think of these three aspects of our personality as an interconnected circle. Each of these aspects is influenced by the other two and together, to paraphrase Pogo, "they is us." In order to bring about change you must make entry into the circle. Behavior provides the best doorway because we can make a conscious decision to change our behavior and this new behavior will have an immediate impact on the way we think and feel. Recall Leon Festinger's cognitive dissonance theory.[24]

# Behavior

# Thoughts      # Feelings

---

23   Ziglar, 1982.
24   Festinger, Leon, *A Theory of Cognitive Dissonance*, Stanford University Press, Palo Alto, CA, 1957.

Thoughts are a second entry point but a much more difficult one. We can and do think many different things and they do have an accumulative impact on our feelings and our behavior, but only slowly, over much time. The human imagination is so limitless that it is difficult to focus our thinking to the point that it will have an immediate impact on our personality. Does this mean what we think is unimportant? Not at all. It is imperative for our long-term health that we think positive thoughts and this should be a vital part of our strategy, but thoughts will seldom have the same immediacy as behavior in bringing about positive change in our ego.

On the other hand, negative thoughts can have a dramatic, deleterious impact. Negative thoughts are pollutants that have a poisonous effect on the system. If the negative thought patterns become habituated, the long-term cumulative effect is staggering. While positive thoughts are important, their impact, unfortunately, is not nearly as dramatic as the negative. It might be helpful to think of positive thinking as a type of preventive maintenance in that it may effectively keep the system from eroding. Negative thoughts are abrasives that do damage.

Finally, feelings offer the poorest entry point because few of us have much, if any, control over what we feel. Our feelings seem to flow from deep within our subconscious mind. Because we are human we feel the full range of emotion, but we are often at a loss to explain why we feel what we do, when we do. It is virtually impossible to turn on feelings whenever we wish and it is unlikely that we can consciously program our feelings to fit our immediate purpose.

Where we can impact for the long term is through entry into the circle via the most accessible point—through our behavior. Of the three aspects it is behavior over which we have the most control. As we change our behavior to the point that a pattern develops, it begins to slowly color the way we think and as we begin to think differently we gradually begin to feel differently. The way our brain works is that it develops a seemingly infinite number of patterns of synaptic connections. As new stimuli are received, the brain works to fit the new information into the existing patterns or connections. By behaving repeatedly in new ways we are actually prompting our brains to form new synaptic patterns. In our brain, recency is primacy.

Interestingly, the brain does not unlearn the old patterns, they simply fall into disuse. It is much like old highway patterns that are replaced by new interstate highway systems. The old roads and intersections do not necessarily disappear they are just less well-traveled.

The new patterns gain primacy over the old ones and they begin to influence not only other behaviors, but also our thoughts and feelings. Our brains, like so many other systems, strive for equilibrium. If our behavior disturbs that equilibrium the system must adjust. If that behavioral change is consistent, equilibrium can only be restored by adjustments to our thoughts and emotions.

As with every other human endeavor, we must begin with the things over which we have control. Clearly behavior is the best vehicle.

**PRESCRIPTION FOR A POSITIVE LIFE**

In order to impact on your self-esteem we recommend a three-part strategy. The first part is an aggressive action strategy directed toward changing your behavior, the second is to develop a portfolio of positive thinking tools, and the final component is to accept our feelings for what they are. We will deal with each in its turn.

**Behavior**

Begin with an acknowledgement that our self-concept is not what we want it to be. Begin, like one begins to deal with any problem, by accepting responsibility for the problem. Remember that it is not until one accepts responsibility for a problem that he acquires the power to solve it. Accept that it is an esteem deficiency, not bad fortune or other external forces, that is at the root of most of the problems, setbacks, and disappointments we experience. Make a commitment to work on your ego and to devote countless hours to its development, much like the golf professional practices his or her swing thousands upon thousands of times in order to eliminate the imperfections and to build permanent muscle memory. It is an incredibly difficult task and takes enormous dedication but the rewards are also incredible. When you find yourself struggling, it is vital that you seek objective assistance just as the golfer turns to his or her instructor, because aberrations in our behavior, which produce the undesirable results, may be virtually invisible to us. This assistance may come from the support of a loved one, a mentor, or the interaction of a professional counselor or therapist.

So what are the steps for changing your self-concept to one that is strong and vibrant and that will give you the strength of character to face the challenges of life?

The first thing is to take stock of who you are. Clear a day for yourself and devote it to self-examination. During this day, make a list of all the things about yourself that you can think of that you like and that other people would like if they knew you. Make the list as exhaustive as you can and then type it up so you will have a clean copy you can keep for daily reference. But, before you put it aside, study it for a while.

If you have been totally honest with yourself it will be a pretty long list. Revel in it for a while and enjoy the view as you would your newly polished car. Admit it to yourself, "I'm a pretty nice person." Shut out any negative thoughts for a while and just take some time to enjoy being you. It's perfectly okay to smile while you're doing this—in fact it is recommended! It's a pretty, shiny thing, isn't it? There is much to feel good about and much about which you can feel proud. So, go ahead and feel good and concentrate on those positives.

Now, as we begin to turn our attention to our imperfections, hang on to the positive feeling and look at your imperfections, not as a cancer that destroys our positive attitude, but merely as a wonderful opportunity to improve who you are—it is just like waxing and polishing your car to remove the blemishes that develop over time.

Next, make a list of those things about you with which you are not pleased. Do not linger on them, but be as honest and objective with yourself as you can. Remember, your entire future depends on this. Resist the temptation to stop short and Do not worry if you begin to feel discouraged or depressed, it's only natural during this phase of the exercise and it is transitory. You are just looking closely for blemishes that need a little buffing.

When the list is complete, write in big bold letters across the top:

### "My little imperfections"

And, that is all these things are—little imperfections. Now, go through your list with a red pen and circle the five items that concern you the most and write them, one each, at the top of five index cards. These represent your immediate objectives; the things about yourself that you most want to improve. Then, on each index card write a short action plan—a list of the specific things you can do, now, to improve your "Little Imperfections." Action plans are a powerful weapon in the arsenal of positive leaders and we will discuss them at great length in a later chapter on the process of success.

Carry these cards around with you and every day, work on those things—not think about doing them but actually doing them. It is okay to think about things; in fact I recommend it. But remember, action is what makes things happen and our behavior is our ticket to a new future. Action is the key to success and it is what separates winners from losers. Action is what distinguishes men and women with vibrant, positive egos from men and women whose egos are weak and fragile.

But Do not just read this and nod your head. Do it! Take action now! Start each day with a positive attitude exercise. First thing each morning, look in the mirror and smile at yourself. That's right! Smile at yourself. It is vital to our objective that you like yourself and, further, that you feel comfortable liking yourself. Think about what you do when you are walking down the street or through a shopping mall and you run into someone whom you know and like. Without even thinking about it, you smile at them. When we like people we smile at them. Smiling is a spontaneous act that reflects that which we feel, so smile at yourself. Do this even if you Do not feel like smiling. Remember that the way we begin to change what we think and feel is to change our behavior because it is the easiest for us to control. If you make smiling in the mirror a daily practice, in fact, if you smile at yourself at every opportunity—as silly as this may sound to you initially—it will begin to impact on the way you feel about yourself. It is truly magical.

Next, be thankful for the day you are about to experience. Take stock of your blessings, including the people who are important to you and also give thanks for your strengths and pay homage to them.

Then, reaffirm your values—the things in which you believe—and renew your commitment to your mission and the specific objectives that define that mission.

Next, acknowledge yourself. "I'm okay! I like who I am. I am not perfect but each day I grow and I learn more about myself and about the world around me. I do not worry about the past. I cannot change the things that occurred yesterday. I can, however, do something about today and what I do here and now will determine much about tomorrow. I concentrate on the things over which I have the power to control and that is what I do today. By doing so, my dreams for the future may become a reality.

Finally, think about the day that awaits you and—in broad strokes—outline in your mind the things you hope to accomplish. Review the five little imperfections that you wrote on index cards and begin thinking about the specific things you will do, each and every day, to implement the action plans you recorded on each card.

This entire ritual should take no more than ten to fifteen minutes of each day but it may well be the most important minutes you will spend all day.

Now, take some deep breaths and give thanks for being alive in this wonderful world in which we live and begin a twenty to thirty minute exercise program geared for your health and physical conditioning. Exercise is a wonderful action tool offering many benefits:

1. It keeps the body healthy and in good physical condition;
2. It gives you the physical energy you require to stay productive all day;
3. It helps maintain a positive attitude; and,
4. It helps combat depression.

Make exercise a regular part of your daily routine and you will never regret the time invested.

Next, have a healthy breakfast and read the paper or watch the morning news. It is important to start the day off with a nutritional meal and it is also important to keep up with current events. Positive people avoid isolation and are full-fledged participants in the real world and so, also, must you be.

Start doing things differently, whatever they are. This part takes real courage and dedication. Forge ahead in the face of all of your fears and anxieties. This is an important opportunity in your life, a chance to do something courageous, to be a hero—to experience "that one moment in time" about which each of us has dreamt at some point in our life.

As you polish off each of your little imperfections ritualize the process of moving an item from your list of little imperfections to the list of things about which you feel good. Then select another imperfection from your list and prepare another action plan to carry with you. Periodically repeat the self-evaluation process. It is always a good thing to look back and contemplate how far we have come and how much we have grown. This reflection also helps us to recalibrate our systems and make sure we have not drifted away from our core purpose and objectives.

Pay close attention now! This is incredibly important. If you do these things faithfully, day in and day out, your life will never be the same. You will begin to feel good about being you and you will begin to discover the incredible power that comes with a healthy sense of self.

Once you have taken control of your own destiny you will learn one of the greatest secrets of life: the only limits that constrain us in life are the limits that exist in our own mind. A healthy human being who believes in himself; who is willing to work hard; and, who gives freely of herself can accomplish almost anything he or she can imagine.

**Positive Thinking**

The generation-old adage common to early data processing environments, "garbage in—garbage out," has great applicability to us. It is as true as true can be that if we continually take in negative thoughts we will live a negative life. Think about your own life for a moment. Do you live in a positive world full of positive thoughts or do you reside in the negative?

For most of us, of course, the answer is that we straddle both worlds. What particularly concerns us is the tendency that most men and women have of grossly under-estimating the impact of the negative portion of our lives and behavior. As you examine your own lives, try to be honest with yourself as you answer the following questions:

1. Are you often frightened of the world?
2. Do you find it difficult to be friendly with people with whom you disagree?
3. Do you feel a lot of anger when things do not go well for you?
4. Do you spend much time dreaming about things you wish you could accomplish but cannot?
5. Do you often dream of instant good fortune, of winning the lottery, for example?
6. Are there many people whom you dislike?
7. Do you complain much about the problems in society?
8. Do you have phobias?
9. Do you feel envy in response to the good fortune of others?
10. Do you find it difficult to start projects or activities?
11. Do you find it difficult to finish what you have started?

This is just a small portion of a list of symptoms of negative-oriented living. If you answer yes to more than one or two of these questions then your life is disproportionately influenced by negativism. If you truly wish, you can do something about your negativism. If you find yourself overwhelmed by negativism and/or you often contemplate ending your life then you are urged to seek professional help. Life need not be a burden and as difficult as it may seem to you now, seeking professional intervention is an incredibly small price to pay for a life of joy. Whether you need professional intervention or not, there are some things you can do on your own that will help you acquire a positive attitude.

Earlier we spoke of Viktor Frankl, who wrote that man's life is spent in search of meaning.[25] Meaning in life varies from person to person, therefore specificity is difficult. The central theme of meaning is that each of us needs to feel that our existence is important and that we have something meaningful to contribute to other people, to life, and to the world.

Questions of the importance of our very existence can only be answered by examining our concept of creation and relationship to the creative force of the universe. This is a very personal thing and the answer that works for one may not work for another. For our purpose, what is vital is that each of us acknowledges the importance, to our very life and happiness, of those things in which we believe.

Our position is simple. Whatever your religious beliefs, they are an important part of what and who you are as a person. The faith which you possess, whatever its genesis, provides a foundation of meaning—a context, if you will—upon which your life is built.

Everyone believes in something, if not God, then something else. As much as I might wish to persuade you that my belief is the correct one, you also would like to persuade me. As humans, we are all striving to make sense of the world and our life and we all strive to understand the mysteries of the universe. Our perception of it is imperfect and our wisdom, however proud we may be of it, is finite. The creation, on the other hand, is vast and infinitely transcends our ability to comprehend.

Each of us experiences a unique relationship with the creative force of the universe, a relationship filtered through our unique personality and seasoned by the degree of comprehension we possess of the world. We each try to understand the meaning of life in the context of this relationship. For some, the relationship is a denial, for others an affirmation. For many it is a combination of denial and affirmation.

---

25  Frankl, 1975.

If that belief gives us faith and strength then we are able to live fully and to prosper in the security of that relationship. With all of our limitations and human imperfections, we take comfort in the knowledge that our life has meaning. This faith gives us strength and the confidence needed for a positive existence. It is vital, therefore, that whatever your beliefs, whatever your relationship with the Creator, put your faith in it and it will give you great power to enjoy rather than to fear life.

Fear is a debilitating emotion and joy is an enabling emotion. Fear causes you to draw yourself inward and away from the world, its people, and its challenges while joy enables you to reach out to the world and its people with the full knowledge that nothing in the world can do harm to your spirit, to your humanity. There is nothing that the world or its people can do to diminish your worth as an individual human being, as a child of Creation.

From these core values, we can build a positive approach to life. As we teach ourselves to think positively our whole attitude changes and our life begins to change as well. If we have been working diligently on our behavior, as well, our separate efforts will begin to supplement each other and the changes we experience will be dramatic—it will be transformational.

**Feelings**

Feelings offer the most difficult entry into the circle but there are strategies that can impact, nevertheless. Our approach in this venue, however, is much subtler. We cannot control our feelings, that much is certain. What we can do, however, is to accept them honestly. Feelings are neither good nor bad. All human beings experience the full range of emotion from love and joy to hate and despair. Most of us deny the negative feelings and experience guilt because of them and we tend to mask them, to hide them from the people in our lives. We have the mistaken impression that our feelings are somehow unique and unnatural, that no one else feels what we feel.

The message of this book is to encourage you to accept the whole range of emotion as natural. You need not feel guilty about what you feel but you must pay attention to your feelings and let them be a catalyst for action.

Whenever we experience anger or hate or any of the other emotions that we consider negative, it is neither an indictment nor is it evidence of pathology. Quite the contrary, it is simply a testament to our humanity. If we accept those emotions for what they are, we can significantly reduce the control they exert on our behavior. Often, when these feelings are exposed to the light of day they turn out to be much less evil and horrible than we imagine.

Conversely, we can benefit immensely by wearing our positive emotions where the world can see. These feelings, like our talents and abilities, are best utilized in the full light of day where they can be shared and serve as a guiding example to those whom we influence.

Acceptance of our range of emotion as evidence of our humanness will enhance our self-esteem. The inner feelings of inadequacy and of not measuring up to other people will be properly put to rest when we compare ourselves objectively with other men and women who feel most of the same things that we feel.

As we dedicate ourselves to changing the way we act, think, and feel the efforts complement one another and real change occurs; change that we will sense in every conceivable way. The whole world around us will appear more beautiful and full of opportunities and the people in that world will seem to smile at us. They will also appear to be less frightening or intimidating.

In possession of a strong sense of self, we can embrace life and all of its vicissitudes from a rock-solid foundation. We discover that there is little to fear in life and, absence of fear means freedom to lead. We become free to reach out to people, to share our ideas and feelings, to take action, and to take a stand. If we choose to exercise that freedom we become positive leaders and the world will be indelibly altered.

## *five*

## UNDERSTANDS ORGANIZATIONS

*"I shall study and prepare myself and some day my chance will come."*
— Abraham Lincoln

*"As they, while others slept, struggled upward in the night."*
— Thoreau

*"Act boldly and unseen forces will come to your aid."*
— Dorthea Brand

Mastery of applied organizational theory is as vital to the success of leadership as knowledge of the piano is to the accomplished pianist. Organizations are the medium in which men and women function in society—they are the playing fields of life and business.

Positive leaders understand organizations in all of their complexity and are accomplished artists in macro- and micro-organizational theory. Most managers possess, or at least utilize, only a rudimentary understanding of organizations. They are like novice personal computer users. They can stumble their way through a few application programs but their lack of in-depth understanding of the computer and its software keeps them from using more than a fraction of the machine's capability. Occasionally, they actually threaten or damage the system by utilizing it improperly or counter-productively.

At the macro level, the positive leader is a student of organizational theory and devotes a significant amount of time keeping up with the literature of the field. At the micro level, he or she is intimately in tune with his or her own organization, with its personality, its subcultures, its metrics, and with its informal power structures. The leader spends a significant amount of time out in the organization, talking and listening and getting involved with people.

In this chapter, we will examine some of the characteristics of organizations and we will look at the challenges organizations present to their leaders. This is complicated subject matter to which we can give only cursory attention. There is a wealth of literature available on organizational theory and the committed positive leader is encouraged to become a student.

## ORGANIZATIONS IN GENERAL

Most human activity takes place in the context of organizations and organizations of all types, shapes, and sizes permeate our existence. We live in organizations (families), play in organizations (clubs or teams), learn in organizations (schools), worship in organizations (churches, synagogues and mosques), work in organizations (business enterprises), volunteer for some organizations (committees and not-for-profits), and we vote and pay taxes to support organizations (governments). Our lives are literally interwoven in a complicated fabric of organizations.

Organizations can range from the incredibly large and complex to the very small and relatively simple. Similar forces, however, govern all.

All organizations are formed to serve some purpose. A couple—an organization with two individuals—is the simplest but even it can be complicated and rife with problems, as so many men and women would attest. Let us examine the couple briefly. It may be a friendship, a romance, a marriage, or some other form of partnership. Why do individuals form such partnerships? The answer, of course, is to achieve a purpose of one kind or another.

In friendships, the partners feel a certain bond and in forming the friendship they are able to achieve a quality of life that is not possible for an individual by him or herself. The two support one another; provide each other with companionship, and all of the other things that accompany friendship. The friendship begins to take on a life of its own according to the needs and contributions of the parties. In that relationship, the partners both give and receive benefit. Ideally, the partners give equally to the relationship and share equally in the benefits. Of course, in the real world the ideal rarely exists and in most relationships the give and take between partners is unequal; fluctuating back and forth.

The relationships, instead, achieve a sort of equilibrium where the partners give and receive at a level that, while not equal, is acceptable to both individuals according to their perceptions of each others' needs and contributions. These same things occur in larger organizations, irrespective of scale.

The character of the organization is determined by the manner in which it meets the needs of its members. Leaders of strong, positive organizations recognize that the entity's effectiveness in meeting its members needs directly influence the level of commitment of the people to the organization's mission, vision, values, and goals. For every primary agenda there will be several secondary agendas. This is particularly true in business organizations to which we now shift our focus.

What do people expect from organizations? We want and expect our organizations to meet our:

- **Material needs** – the business organization must afford its people with a living wage and compensation package, one that is perceived as a fair and equitable exchange for each individual's contributions.
- **Need for identity and esteem** – the organization must be a winner, one that gives the individual a feeling of pride of belonging. It must contribute positively to their self-esteem.
- **Need for affiliation** – it must bring the individual into contact with other people in a way that enables the formation of friendships. People are social creatures and jobs have become the community—the general store in which people gather.
- **Need for achievement** – People strive for a sense of accomplishment. For a feeling that their life has meaning and importance; that the work they perform has intrinsic value.

- **Need for power** – people need to feel that they have some power or control over their lives and their destiny. Nothing contributes to hopelessness like powerlessness and nothing is more pathetic than a hopeless soul.
- **Need for security** – people need to feel secure in their relationships at all levels, both personal and organizational. Security is founded on trust. The only way the individual can feel secure is when they trust the organization and its leadership.

People can meet these needs in the formal activity and mainstream culture of the organization or in the informal activity or a subculture. Where these needs are met is almost always the consequence of the quality of leadership provided to the organization. And clearly, the degree to which the needs of an organization's people are met will determine the level of effort and commitment people will give to an organization's purpose.

Positive leaders work hard to create a positive organization, one that meets the needs of each of its people. As a result, these organizations are energized, vibrant, productive, innovative, and profitable.

What do organizations need? Organizations require a cooperative effort from their people, which is just another way of saying teamwork. Teamwork is the key to the success of any organization.

People are the most important resource of any organization. Organizations require that people understand its mission and that they share a commitment to that mission. For what purpose does our organization exist? Are we, the organization's members, ready to make sacrifices for that purpose or mission? Organizations require people who have faith and who pledge their allegiance.

Organizations also require leadership:

- that incessantly focuses the organization's attention to its mission, vision, and values and on the specific goals and objectives that have been developed to carry out that mission.
- that is fully committed to the mission and that will tolerate little deviation from that purpose.

- that will communicate with every individual in the organization, providing feedback on their performance and clarification of expectations:
  - that will provide positive feedback to positive performances,
  - that will take positive action in response to unsatisfactory outcomes.
- that will turn its back on nothing, especially the values of the organization.

Organizations require leadership that will continually ask questions and leadership that will challenge its assumptions about everything, all of the time. They need leaders who fear complacency above all else and who believe that the point at which an idea, process, product, or service can no longer be improved is the precise moment in time that it becomes obsolete.

Organizations require leadership that continually communicates with the entity's public; with the people and markets served by its products or services. They require leaders who listen to the people and to the marketplace, who understand that the needs of the marketplace are paramount and that they are both dynamic and fluid.

Organizations require clearly defined value systems and leaders who constantly redefine those values and are fully and irrevocably committed to their practice.

Nothing weakens organizations more than leaders who do not enforce the value system of the organization zealously and diligently. As I talk with employees in my role as a management consultant, one of the most frequent complaints I hear is that management does little about the people who fail to carry their share of the burden. Few things are as frustrating as the feeling that we are the only person in the organization to work hard and nothing will stop people from working hard more quickly than this.

"Why should I bust my tail when no one else does and when nobody up front cares?"

The other common source of frustration is that "management is always preaching about quality but does not hesitate to sacrifice quality themselves when it is convenient to do so."

Effective leaders border on compulsiveness in that they are relentless in their efforts to stamp out shoddy effort or performance. They are tireless and single minded. The key, however, is to be demanding in a positive way. Is this possible? The answer is that it is not only possible, it produces astonishing results.

One of the quick and dirty tests you can employ to evaluate the quality of the leadership you provide is to ask yourself two questions. Better yet, let someone ask these questions of your people:

12. Are you an easy mark, quick to back down on demands for quality?
13. Are your people afraid to make mistakes?

A "Yes" response to either question suggests that your leadership style is weak and ineffective.

Effective leaders are relentless in their demand for the best efforts of their people and in pursuit of the highest expectations. The degree of effort required is non-negotiable. Positive leaders also understand that people make mistakes when they extend themselves, when they reach into uncharted territory. These men and women view mistakes as proof of effort and perfect opportunities to learn. Mistakes are like a fall to a skier. A good ski instructor would teach that if you are not falling down once in a while, you are not really skiing. Mistakes are celebrated! With each error, minor adjustments are made until we have it just right. Then, we are ready to move on to more difficult challenges.

How does leadership accomplish these things? They do so by being totally and unreservedly committed to doing them. What leaders must do is spend their time doing those things that are most important; things that only they can do. The things that are important begin with talking to the people of the organization, constantly. What do you talk about? You talk about the mission, about quality, about goals and objectives, about expectations, about teamwork, about customer satisfaction, about new ideas, about finding ways to do the job better and with less friction. Friction is the byproduct of inefficiency and is measured from both a fiscal and an emotional perspective. Leaders give continuous, ongoing feedback on how their people are doing. Counting things that are important is a powerful tool because what you count are outcomes of activity. Outcomes are impersonal and are neither threatening nor demeaning. The numbers are what they are.

Positive leaders also spend time listening to the people in their organization. Remember always that communication must flow in all directions, both inward and outward and up and down. Effective leaders are accomplished listeners. They believe in people and they understand one of the most flattering things one can do is to listen to what people have to say. It is the most powerful form of positive reinforcement and the only cost is the leader's time and attention.

What do we mean by positive and active listening? It means that you respond to people and acknowledge them. That you act on what they have to say. That you empathize with their concerns and when those concerns are legitimate, you take appropriate action or, better yet, you empower your people to take appropriate action. When people on your team have a good idea, you facilitate its implementation and make certain they get all the credit they deserve.

Once you have established a pattern of empathic listening and of making things happen in response, you have helped three powerful and positive things happen. You have established both credibility and precedent and you have laid the foundation for loyalty.

Let's discuss credibility first. When we speak of credibility we are really talking about trust. An atmosphere of trust is an essential component of healthy, creative, and high-performing organizations. Trust is a miraculous thing. When it exists, the limits to the potential of the organization have been expanded exponentially. Organizations characterized by an atmosphere of trust can accomplish almost anything because its people are willing to extend themselves. They are willing to take risks. They have no fear of failure and they trust that leadership will express its appreciation in meaningful ways. The latter may occasionally refer to compensation, but it always means recognition and respect.

In trusting organizations, it is okay for leadership to ask its people for extraordinary efforts and sacrifices during difficult and challenging times because the people have faith in leadership's ability and integrity. They know they will not be taken advantage of, exploited unfairly, or abused in any way. People also know that their leaders are there to help when needed.

In trusting organizations it is not only okay for leaders to take decisive action in response to inefficiency or unacceptable effort, it is desired and expected.

How do leaders build this level of trust? It is not that difficult if the leadership has integrity. When a leader lacks integrity building trust is impossible. Every positive leader must demonstrate his or her integrity every day, with every action, and with every word. Actions establish precedents, living proof that the employees' trust in them is merited. There is no such thing as a little integrity. One either possesses integrity or one does not. When integrity is accepted as a given, people will be prepared to pledge their loyalty.

Believe in the mission of the organization and make absolutely certain that your mission is positive. Erect a value system around the mission, a value system that encourages and rewards behavior that contributes to the mission and which is totally intolerant of behavior that undermines the mission.

Talk about that mission and value system at every opportunity and never, ever pass up an opportunity to do so. If your people do not know what you are going to say then you do not say it with sufficient frequency. Your primary job as a leader is to sell your mission, share your vision of the future, and to teach your values. Literally, talking about your mission, vision, and the organization's values should consume a minimum of fifty percent of your time. If you are not doing that now, you are not doing your job.

This is also not a job you can do while sitting in your office or when your time is consumed by administrative tasks. In fact, there are very few important things that can be accomplished from one's desk or office.

Often leaders, while hiding in their offices, brag about their open-door policy. The problem with open-door policies is that they work best when it's the manager leaving the office to go out into the plant rather than people entering their boss's office. The barriers to the manager or supervisor's office are far more imposing than a door. Even in the most trusting organization, only a small percentage of the people will cross the barrier to seek out their boss on an issue that troubles them. Managers who wait for their people to come to them will never talk, meaningfully, to a substantial portion of their workforce.

It is also impossible to spend fifty percent or more of your time talking to your people if you are bogged down on bureaucratic nonsense. There is precious little paper work that is as important as face-to-face contact with every man and woman in your organization unless it is a contract, check, or action plan. I have yet to see a piece of paper solve a problem, come up with an innovative idea, increase productivity, clean up a mess, or listen to a customer's complaint. Only people can do these things and these are the only things that count. Paperwork is worthwhile only as a tool to help you accomplish an objective and it must never be allowed to evolve into an end, in and of itself.

If your organization is so large that it is physically impossible to communicate one-on-one with each of your people then, by all means, communicate through other media. But, more importantly, spend your time talking to your leadership team and make certain that each of them is out in the field or plant, talking and listening to their people. After all, your leadership cadre are your ambassadors; they are extensions of you and it is vital that they can speak to mission, vision, and values with the same eloquence as you. Evaluate them on the basis of the time they spend in direct communication with the people of your organization and hold out that same expectation for yourself. Maybe you cannot talk to everyone or with the frequency you would prefer but talk to as many as you are able and do so at every opportunity. It is your job to set the example. If you are insufficiently committed to do it yourself you will never convince your leadership team that you mean business.

By the way, the other fifty percent of a leader's time should be devoted to communication (talking and listening) with the members of your supply chain; your customers and suppliers. Yes, it seems incredible—almost impossible—and few managers come close. We have been taught that a manager's time should be spent planning and preparing reports, budgets, and forecasts. And yes, these activities are vital. What many misunderstand, however, is that these are all things that can not only be delegated but they are also things that are best done with the involvement of one's people while we are talking and listening to them. A leader's face-to-face time with the people of his or her organization, cannot be delegated. The most effective way to complete reports, budgets, forecasts and other such activities is through the full participation of the people of the organization.

The valuable time of leadership must be spent on the things that matter most, the things that only leadership can do effectively. What are these most vital activities? Selling the mission, teaching the values and sharing the vision of the organization and, yes, even authors writing books on the subject of positive leadership must say things with sufficient frequency that you can hear, see, and feel it coming. These are important jobs and when you cannot get it done it is time to expand your leadership team.

Leadership is not, nor has it ever been a one-person job. It may commence with one person but it must be shared with an ever-expanding group of people until virtually every man and woman in the organization is touched by it and understands that they, too, are expected to provide leadership and accept responsibility for the challenges of the organization.

**Trust**

We have already talked about trust but it is so important that we need to give it further attention. Lack of confidence and mistrust begin very subtly. Most people join an organization with hope and optimism and are fully prepared to trust in their leadership if they can see any reason at all to do so.

What often happens, however, is that the leadership they receive is dull and uninspiring. Many managers and supervisors display a negative attitude, complain about being bogged down in paperwork and, they badmouth the organization and upper management. These men and women complain that no one listens to them, take the attitude that there is nothing that can be done, that the situation is hopeless. They turn their backs on problems in their own units and avoid problems and responsibility for the things that do occur.

Each of these occurrences or symptoms sends a clear message to the people of the organization, that their leaders are powerless and without courage. Who in their right mind can have confidence in a leader who lacks both power and courage? The result is an environment lacking in positive, effective leadership and where people pay precious little attention to anything management says or does.

Sadly, few managers understand what they have lost. Neither are they willing to accept responsibility for its absence. These ineffectual leaders think of themselves as victims and they do not see how their own actions, or lack of action, have contributed to the very problems about which they complain. In their self-induced state of powerlessness, they are unable to see that they have the power to bring about radical, positive changes—that they can turn the situation around. Situations like this offer wonderful opportunities for leaders and anyone with an action-oriented, positive approach can do wonders and, in the process, come out looking like both a genius and a hero; in full possession of the trust and loyalty of the organization and its people.

Begin by letting your people know that you have a vision for the organization; that you know exactly what needs to be done; that you know how to go about it; that you are fully prepared to start immediately, with a total commitment; and, that you need their help and participation. This is how you build trust. Through your actions, demonstrate that people can have confidence in what you do and say. If you must ask for the trust of your people, then something has gone terribly wrong. Share your vision with them, often. In fact, never let an opportunity pass you by to share your vision of the organization with your people. Say it at every formal gathering and meeting and in every informal conversation with your people as you wander through your business. If they do not know what you intend to say, then you are not saying it with sufficient frequency. [A note to the reader: hopefully this will explain why I seem to be repeating myself in this book.]

One of the things people most often want from their leadership is a sense of direction and a confidence that the leadership will find a way to make things work. This creates hope. Hope creates confidence. Confidence creates security, and security creates an atmosphere that engenders creativity and risk-taking.

In the 1992 NCAA Basketball Final Four, in what has become college basketball lore, defending champion Duke University was trailing with 2.8 seconds to go in the game. They had possession and had to bring the ball the full length of the court. After winning the game, Coach Mike Krzyzewski was asked what he told his players during the time out. He responded, "The first thing I told them was that we were going to win the game." Recognized as one of the premier coaches in college athletics, Coach K knew that victory was contingent upon his ability to instill in the minds of his players the belief that winning was not only a possible outcome, it was the expected outcome. All that remained was to explain to them how it would be accomplished.

People in an organization are like citizens of a city, state, or nation. They want to know that their leaders are winners and that positive outcomes are the expectation. Men and women also want to know that their leaders will take care of problems and will discipline rule-breakers and troublemakers. Few things are as frustrating as the sense of injustice we feel when we believe we have been treated unfairly or when someone else reaps the benefits of our hard work. Leaders who respond promptly to these inequities immediately earn the respect and trust of their people.

It is this willingness and ability to be a proactive, action-oriented leader that tends to build trust. On the other side of the ledger, who can have confidence in a loser or in a wimp? Wishy-washy, indecisive managers (they certainly are not leaders) contribute much to an atmosphere of mistrust and suspicion and to muddied visions and poorly clarified value systems.

The most important thing to remember about organizations, regardless of their size and complexity, is that they were formed for a specific reason or purpose. This reason or purpose—this mission—is the thing that drives the organization and bestows legitimacy. Even the largest organizations in the world, nation-states, have a clear and distinct mission. For example, as all Americans should know, The United States of America exists to serve and protect its people in the context of personal liberty. Everything our government does, every action it takes, can and must be evaluated on the basis of how its actions contribute to the fulfillment of that mission.

Business entities are no different. Each has a distinct purpose or mission that relates to how it will serve its customers. The mission is not, as many believe, to make money. Yes, business organizations must make money if they wish to survive and prosper but making money is not the mission of the organization. The only organizations that truly exist to make money are government mints and currency printing houses.

Peter Drucker presents this idea in his famous work, *Management: Tasks, Responsibilities, Practices*.[26] Drucker suggests that businesses do not exist to make money but rather to satisfy customers. The leaders who forget the mission of their organizations and who conduct business in a manner that places making money ahead of satisfying customers are on their way to trouble. These operations sacrifice long-term customer satisfaction for short-term profits. Inevitably, this lack of focus results in loss of market share as unhappy customers seek out alternate suppliers. Organizations that are distracted from their purpose lose their customers and, therefore, lose money in the long-run.

---

26   Drucker, 1974.

Successful business ventures are measured over the long-term. Those enterprises that maintain their focus on customer satisfaction, even if it occasionally means absorbing short-term losses, will win in the long run through solidification of its market share. Satisfied customers will keep coming back and the reputation for keeping customers satisfied will bring more customers. One of the consequences of keeping one's customers satisfied is that they remain willing to pay money for what we do. As a result, we do make money and our investors do receive a return on their investment. It would be a rare customer who would elect to pay us just because we asked them to do so, or because we promised to deliver a product or service if we got their money. Almost always, the customer will pay willingly only when satisfied that the product or service meets or exceeds their expectations.

It is almost universally true that organizations that are struggling have gravitated to secondary agendas that may overlook or even conflict with the mission of customer satisfaction. Once the downhill slide has begun, it is a precipitous process, one that is difficult to reverse. For this reason, it is vital that leaders insure that their organization's mission is clearly understood by all and that every dollar and every ounce of energy expended are directed toward serving that mission.

How is this done and who is responsible? The answer should come as no surprise. This vital responsibility rests with leadership. One of the most important jobs of leadership is to keep the organization and its people on course. Leaders who take this to heart are eminently successful. Positive leaders do this best of all!

One of the biggest mistakes leaders make is a failure to recognize subtle changes in a customer's requirements. This occurs when people become complacent and when they assume too much. These individuals stop listening and assume they know the answers because they think today's answers will be the same as were yesterday's. Everything in life is in a state of constant change and business is no different. There is a tendency, in human beings, to hang on to that with which they are comfortable. We have all heard them. "That's the way we've always done it!" These men and women are probably correct but that doesn't change the reality that the world is changing around us, as we speak. It is unfortunate that, for many businesses, it is not until they lose a long-standing customer that they are willing to step back and challenge their organization's assumptions. In many cases this is too late. Subtly or not, the needs of our customers' change and we must be vigilant in our efforts to listen, observe, and adapt what we do to meet those dynamic requirements.

**Values**

From its mission and purpose the organization naturally begins to form values. These values represent what is considered right and wrong in the organization and what is good and bad. Successful winning organizations inevitably embrace positive values. Leadership is challenged to live those values with unyielding enthusiasm and consistency. A few examples of such values might include such things as quality, hard work, honesty, commitment to customer satisfaction, pride, teamwork, positive recognition and reinforcement, respect, and many more. Everything leadership does and every decision leadership makes reflects these values and all outcomes are measured within the context of these most essential values.

Never are values to be sacrificed. To do so would unravel the whole value-system and irrevocably damage the credibility of leadership, which in turn destroys trust. It is the very same challenge parents face with their children. As a parent, you can talk all your want but your actions speak most eloquently and they reflect that which you hold dear. You can talk about hard work but it is meaningless when you turn your back on their half-hearted effort. You can talk about discipline but until you teach your children and colleagues the importance of discipline and hold them to high standards, your words are just talk. You can talk about quality all you want at your company but you will convince no one when you demonstrate a willingness to sacrifice quality for the sake of expediency.

Leadership must be committed to its values and must display its loyalty to those values even when doing so is difficult. The people of an organization expect their leaders to be strong and consistent and the people will respect the leaders that are. Managers and supervisors who lose that respect no longer function effectively as leaders. Leaders are expected to have the courage of their convictions.

Leaders who display these attributes can be as tough as leather and as demanding as can be. They are always fair, however, and always consistent. Each and every individual in the organization knows what to expect and what is expected of them. They know what is valued and what is not. In high energy organizations led by positive leaders the people know what their leader is going to say because the leader never passes up an opportunity to share their vision, sell the mission, teach the values, and clarify expectations.

If these men and women are positive leaders, they also never miss an opportunity to share the glory and the credit for a job well done with each and every member of the organization. Positive leaders are winners and they want every member of their team to be a winner.

**Teamwork**

One of the values that has unparalleled importance to the success of winning organizations is teamwork. In the context of the Theory of Positive Leadership, teamwork is pretty well defined. It means all of the players sharing responsibility for performance, for ideas, for decision-making and, also, for sharing in the rewards of victory. Teamwork means accepting a role because success and recognition come from the team's performance. Teamwork may even mean making personal sacrifices—giving of oneself to the mission and its objectives.

Teamwork is, in fact, the only kind of behavior that consistently produces positive, long-term results in a group or organizational setting. Other approaches, featuring the individual, may have moments of glory but success cannot be achieved over time without team effort. Effective leaders understand this at both the intellectual and emotional level and they never pass up the opportunity to talk about teamwork, to teach teamwork, to reward teamwork, and to sell the concept of teamwork. It is one of the core values of the organization and it is sacrificed for no one, nowhere, and at no time.

Not surprisingly, building teamwork requires that leadership play the role of coach. It requires mapping out a game plan, assigning responsibilities, teaching fundamentals, clarifying and re-clarifying roles and responsibilities, teaching unselfishness, putting the team through its paces with drills and practices and more drills and practices. It requires demanding a consistent level of performance and asking team members to sacrifice themselves to the task. And, this is still insufficient. For the team to be a winning team, the coach must give it a schedule of challenges through which the team can experience and then celebrate victory.

Teamwork not only requires leadership from the sidelines from the coaching staff but also requires leadership from the field of play. The individual members of a team must be taught that it is their responsibility to provide leadership whenever it seems needed; to encourage, praise, push, and even coach their teammates whenever they see the need. There must be no abdication of responsibility by anyone, for anything.

**Bureaucracy**

One of the problems with business organizations, big and small, is that as they grow in size and complexity, they become bureaucratic. They devote an ever-increasing portion of their time and energy to serving and maintaining the corporate structure and proportionately less effort to their mission. What will emerge in such situations are secondary agendas that, not uncommonly, conflict with the objective of producing quality products and services.

It usually begins the same way. The small business has become so successful that in order to meet the expanding demands of customers, it must add capacity. As both the size of staff and the number of customers balloons, the original management team finds themselves unable to handle all of the responsibilities. At this point the company has two options:

- It can add more line staff and delegate more authority so they can discharge the responsibilities effectively and assume more of the leadership burden, or

- They can create more management positions to pick up the slack.

Typically, the second alternative is the alternative of choice. Why? Because "we have added so many people we are not certain as to their capabilities. We really need someone we can count on (trust) to handle the responsibility." We add management staff and guess what? Things resolve. Everything runs more smoothly. Profits surge. Customers are satisfied. Business is booming and everyone is happy.

As the business continues to grow the cycle repeats itself several times over. How do we respond? Well, of course, we are fast learners so we replicate our earlier response and add more management structure. We have also become more sophisticated and countless opportunities emerge to assign specialized roles and responsibilities. We add an accounting department, a computerized management information system, a quality control department, purchasing, marketing, research and development, human resources, planning, etc. And WOW! Great things happen! These people are great at what they do.

We receive sophisticated financial reports, in rich variety. We get the most advanced "statistical process control" systems in the industry. We get innovative marketing strategies, state-of-the-art laboratories, top-of-the-line human resources systems, a full complement of short- and long-range strategic plans, all generated in volumes of computer paper, spewed out by the latest software packages. And once again, great things happen. We are at the top of our industry and we have "market share."

When these departments, so vital to our ongoing success, demand more and more resources that will enable them to duplicate past successes, we show no hesitation. These are the things that got us to where we are today! We make certain that they receive whatever they need to keep us at the top of the mountain. And, by golly, if they need better reports and more cooperation from the production people, from customer service, or sales staff, we let it be known that these departments are working hard to preserve our future and to position us to take advantage of new market opportunities. Whatever they need they damn well better get!

In a few short years we have become a sophisticated corporation. Just when we think we ought to be king of the hill, we begin to see problems on the horizon. If our productivity is increasing at all, it is doing so at a declining rate. We find that our costs have increased in direct and often geometric proportion to our declining productivity. All the while the marketplace is inundated with new products and enhancements from competitors that have seemingly sprung from nowhere, or so it seems; maybe from across town or maybe in China or other far-flung places.

In the face of this erupting pressure, we invest even greater sums in R & D, in larger computer systems, more accountants to crunch the numbers in new and innovative ways, and more planners, and more analysts from the best MBA programs, to devise more sophisticated strategies than ever before. Whatever they need, be it newer equipment or more staff assistance, they get it. And, silently, our costs escalate.

Inevitably, someone suggests a fully automated production line with state-of-the-art robotics as the answer to our spiraling costs. And, of course, it makes perfect sense. After all, look what got us this far. So, on we march into the oblivion of corporate purgatory until the only thing that will salvage our organization is a hostile takeover, followed by a mass sale of our assets and a radical amputation of our bulk; until we have been pared down to small, lean units that have a chance of competing effectively in the marketplace where once we reigned supreme.

Where did we go wrong? We forgot the fundamentals. We lost sight of our mission and we put our faith in systems rather than in people. We allowed, even encouraged, secondary agendas to supplant primary agendas. We erected multiple barriers between our leadership and our most important resource, our people.

It is not impossible to reverse the bureaucratization process but to do so entails radical surgery and will create significant trauma throughout the organization. If this radical surgery is performed by a competent leadership team, the patient will survive and live a more prosperous life.

Of course the best way to eliminate bureaucracy is to avoid it at the outset. In today's economy the most successful companies are lean and energized. Make a commitment in your organizations to take the bureaucracy challenge.

Examine your management and support staff and the resource costs of these functions. How many dollars are spent on these non-revenue producing functions to support your company's bureaucracy? How many dollars are expended on activities that do not provide direct benefit to customers? Examine your administrative overhead. How much is really necessary to support production, sales, service delivery, quality control, and product development. How much is spent to legislate, administer, and adjudicate rules, and on our burgeoning administrative overhead? Look at your line management staff. Evaluate span of control. If it is less than one supervisor to twenty people, compute the incremental cost to sustain a span of control of less than the 1:20 ratio.

Total these costs and they represent the direct cost of your bureaucracy. Then add in the opportunity cost of those dollars (the value of production or sales opportunities lost because those funds were diverted) and compound them over a period of years and you begin to approach the true cost of your bureaucracy. These dollars produce no appreciable benefit to quality, customer service, sales, market penetration, or innovation. Bureaucracies erode profits and sap the energy of your organization by making work more difficult and less enjoyable for the people that do contribute.

Measure the fat content of your enterprise. Many organizations could reduce the money spent on bureaucracy by a quarter to one half. Those resources re-invested in leadership development and remediation, technical training and technology enhancements would produce dramatic increases in quality, productivity, innovation, and customer service.

Every company needs a certain amount of support personnel but most go overboard. After a while, the people that were hired to support the people on the line begin to become entrenched and also lose their focus on their mission. The end result is often that they no longer support and, instead, seem to complicate the production process. Very often, they ask production or sales staff to modify what they are doing to make the work of various administrative staff easier.

Routinely, the important question we should be asking is: who exists to serve whom? If we think of our operation in terms of an internal supply chain we will find it easier to answer the "who exists to serve whom?" question. Supply chains, whether internal or external are interdependent systems. Each link in the supply chain must know not only who exists to serve it but also whom they exist to serve.

Set a goal for your entire team to identify activities or regulations that subvert or impede the production process, and eliminate them. In fact, celebrate such eliminations.

How did these kinds of situations come about? We have spent an entire century on what I refer to as defensive management. Defensive management is guided by a philosophy in which you strive to build perfect organizations with sophisticated control systems that are designed to anticipate administrative or disciplinary problems and then attempts to prevent them on the one hand, and set up a mechanism to resolve them when they occur, on the other. We have relied on advice from management experts whose very premises are outmoded and on attorneys who are concerned, first and foremost, about litigation.

This last point is vital because a good portion of the bureaucracy in any organization exists to prevent law suits that may or may not happen, some day. It is clearly a case where the treatment is far more deadly than the disease. All of this is based on the erroneous assumption that systems solve problems when we have known all along that it is people who solve problems. Systems are tools to be used by people to solve problems, not the other way around.

The lawyers will argue that such systems have saved millions of dollars in litigation. Our question would be, "at what cost?" The sum of the direct cost of these avoidance systems, inefficiencies, bureaucracies, combined with the opportunity costs, is staggering.

The best prevention against lawsuits is so simple that it is often discounted altogether. If you wish to prevent law suits against your company, the secret is to treat your employees fairly, produce quality products and services, and address issues of performance, professionalism, and quality immediately, at the lowest possible level. When the problem is with a valued customer, sit down and work out a solution face to face, eyeball to eyeball.

"Focus on the customer" is rule number one but sometimes people are confused about the identity of their customer. Again, we are talking about supply chain management. To people in support roles the customer is usually the employees in the trenches, whether on the production line, in sales, or at the reception desk. Once again the operative question is, "who exists to serve whom?" Make certain that your customers, whoever they may be, receive first consideration, always. Keep their needs and interests in the forefront of your consciousness and at the top of your priority list.

In some highly regulated industries, as with short- and long-term health care facilities, the customer list may even include governmental regulatory agencies.

The importance of this point cannot be underestimated as a huge proportion of the problems and inefficiencies that exist in business organization flows from this concept—that people in the organization have forgotten whom they exist to serve and even more fundamentally, what it means to serve.

**The Few Rules Theory**

One of the biggest causes of bureaucracy is the theory of management by legislation. Rules and regulations, along with complex policies and procedures, are stifling organizations throughout the economy; literally squeezing the life out of them. Rules and regulations are the genesis of bureaucracies. One of the most important things positive leaders can do for their organizations is to get rid of as many rules as possible.

Yes, I know this sounds radical. While it does represent a radical departure from traditional management/leadership responsibility, it is not nearly as radical as it first appears. In fact, people have long understood that there are too many rules but few have understood that they have the power to do something about the situation, if only they had the courage.

Why so many rules to begin with? There are two reasons:

1. Because most managers elect to solve problems through legislation, rather than face-to-face at the lowest possible level in the organization, and
2. Because of the influence of attorneys on the business of management.

Let's examine them one at a time.

In the first instance, most of us have been taught that the simplest way to solve a problem or to eliminate an undesirable behavior is to create a rule, law or regulation. After all, do we not live in a society governed by the Rule of Law?

While legislation may be necessary and beneficial in the governance of pluralistic societies, it is debilitating to business organizations that generally have a singular mission or purpose. Yes, it may be quite beneficial to have a basic set of guidelines concerning the behavior that is expected of people but this is as far as it goes.

The fact is that most rules are established because a manager lacks the courage to deal with a problem, or a problem employee, face-to-face. Instead, leaders apply the "I'll show you approach" that teaches that if one person abuses the system, punish everyone. This is what happens, after all, when we establish a rule that says "no one can do such and such." It is a real "take charge" thing to do and the action clearly demonstrates the decisiveness and power of the rule maker. After all, one of the things managers have the power to do is to create rules.

Sadly, this approach reinforces all the wrong things. It teaches that management trusts neither themselves nor their people. It results in an atmosphere in which the people who work hard, and do their best to be good employees begin to feel unappreciated. What's the use of working hard to do the best job of which one is capable when the organization does nothing about the people who give less than their best or who create problems for which the rest of us are punished? Such rules teach your people that management is insincere when it says it will crack down on shirkers of responsibility and will look out for the people who do a good job for the organization.

It teaches all the wrong things.

The lesson to be learned is that leaders will not be successful if their solution to a problem is to legislate. Rules do not solve problems, commitment solves problems and people solve problems.

A certain number of rules are inevitable (and probably necessary) in every organization but rules should never be allowed to stand in the way of performance or initiative. That there are too many rules is not some radical new thought. The adage that "rules were made to be broken" has been with us for a very long time.

The evolution of bureaucracies and the spread of rules are parallel phenomena. The following scenario describes the process as it occurs with most companies. As the organization grows it adds more and more people. The more people that are involved in an enterprise, the more problems will be experienced. Many managers are prone to avoid confrontation and the perceived ill-will that can be generated in reaction to that confrontation. Many managers lack the strength of character to stare controversy in the eye and to risk the disfavor of their people. Their avoidance strategy is to create a rule to address future occurrences of the undesirable behavior.

As new problems arise, more rules are promulgated until the number of rules is so great that the company must hire someone to administer compliance. In the meantime, the organization continues to add people and additional rules are enacted. Before long the enforcement officer requires an assistant, and then a secretary and other support staff. The next thing we know, the burden of overhead has grown to accommodate an enforcement department, all at the expense of the bottom line. Rules are the lifeblood of bureaucracy and the anathema of profitability.

Our point is, simply, that very little of this is necessary. Organizations that demand that their management staff accept responsibility for solving problems directly, and at the lowest possible level, are able to avoid this trap. As a result they are lean, responsive, and profitable.

The emotional impact on the organization, resulting from bureaucracy is tremendous. Management solves problems by punishing everyone for the offenses of the few and, in the process, strangles individual enthusiasm and initiative. Inevitably, it is the best employees who pay the price because the transgressors typically don't give a damn!

All organizations have a large, yet finite, pool of energy to power it toward fulfillment of its mission. Like people, organizations utilize only a fraction of their potential energy and a good deal of the energy they expend is squandered on the enactment, publication, and enforcement of unnecessary rules and regulations. Typically these rules and regulations have little or nothing to do with the mission but quickly acquire a level of importance second to none.

We recommend a new approach. Do not listen to your attorneys when it comes to running your business. This sounds dangerous—almost blasphemous—but in actuality it is just common sense. They may be fine lawyers who are doing what they think is best for their clients but they do not know squat about running your business. If left to attorneys, your policy manuals will read like annotated code, require a library to shelve it, and will depend on a staff of lawyers and law clerks to administer—all to prevent the possibility of litigation which may or may not occur, someday. If the law suit happens then let the attorneys do their job and represent you in the court room or courthouse hallways and conference rooms.

Yes, I understand that attorneys preach preventative methods and it seems to make intuitive good sense. After all, isn't prevention the best medicine? The answer may be "Yes" in health care but in a business environment what attorneys call prevention is not really prevention at all. It is avoidance. Prevention is treating people fairly and paying attention to their individual and group needs and interests, and it is properly documenting what is said and done.

The solution is to teach the leaders of your organization how to deal with problems directly, at the lowest possible level, using positive leadership skills. Consistency is the key. If an individual abuses the freedom our employees are given, deal with the abuser and document what happened and how we responded. Teach them that freedom must be balanced by responsibility. If one or more employees are habitually late, Do not toughen up attendance policy. Instead, talk to them face to face and, if they are unwilling to respond, let there be natural consequences for their lack of responsibility and document what was done and how you responded. If an employee consistently shirks their responsibilities, does shoddy work, or fails to carry their fair share of the effort, deal with them as individuals whose performance is unacceptable and document what were the expectations and results and what remedies were employed. These things are the responsibility of leadership.

Such leadership takes courage but courage is one of the pre-requisites of the job. It has always fascinated me how many supervisors and managers are reluctant to deal with problem employees face-to-face and eyeball-to-eyeball because they do not want to be the bad guy or gal. Think about how many times, when you were working with a substandard team member, that you wanted the supervisor to do something about it? How many times did you think of that manager or supervisor as a wimp?

The good and responsible employees will not think of you as a bad guy or gal when you deal with a problem employee who is making their jobs more difficult. In fact, just the opposite is true. They will think of you as a hero. If you are going to worry about what your people will think, worry about what your best employees will think not what the worst ones will think. The people who carry the load, day after day, are the only ones about whom you should be concerned. As far as the problem employee is concerned, take my father's advice. Let marginal or problem employees worry about what you are thinking.

Truly valuing your people and treating them like the precious resource that they are is the best lawsuit prevention strategy in the world. Develop simple, straightforward policies that can be understood by every man and woman in the organization. Ask yourself whether your policies make sense at the gut level.

When action must be taken against a problem employee, document each and every incident and also each and every action that you took in response. Document what expectations were established as a result of such interventions and that all of the parties agreed to accept responsibility for meeting those expectations. Because the behaviors of substandard employees always affects productivity, make use of integrated performance management to document how their productivity suffers and how that affects the performance outcomes of the line, team, or department, all the way up the supply chain.

If such an employee chooses to take legal action, your documentation of exactly what they did and how you responded, each and every step of the way within the context of a set of simple and straightforward policies will provide a much more powerful defense than all of the rules and regulations in the world.

It is necessary to mention government regulations as a good deal of the bureaucracy that we find in the business environment are mandated by government. Although there are certainly issues about which government involvement is needed, our government agencies should be spending most of that energy policing themselves. In our sophisticated world economy, the business enterprise needs to be fast and lean. This requires divestiture of the enormous baggage that so many firms are required to carry in order to comply with regulations. When such regulations are necessary, however, do not fight, complain, or anguish about them and Do not let your people worry about them either. Simply deal with them forthrightly and matter-of-factly as you would any other customer expectation. All such regulatory agencies are nothing more than a specialized form of customer and, hence, a part of your supply chain.

Is regulation, to the extent we have today, really that necessary? The need for regulation is, ultimately, a result the lack of trustworthiness of modern producers of goods and services. Risks are inevitable but, if we are to compete successfully against global competition, we must get to a point at which we are able and willing to trust someone.

We have to demand that leadership rise to the challenge and be trustworthy. Today we trust no one, neither government nor business. It is a symptom of our times that so many of our institutions are deemed untrustworthy. This must change and that change can only come through positive leadership.

**Subcultures**

Bureaucracies are just one example of how secondary agendas can usurp the vital life and productivity of an organization. The larger the organization grows the more subcultures will be spawned because neither the organization as a whole, nor any of its formal subdivisions (divisions, departments, units, teams, lines, task forces, etc.) are adequately meeting the needs of its people.

Since having their needs met is a primary agenda of individuals, they set out to achieve that which the organization does not provide. Individuals establish alliances with other individuals for the purpose of meeting those needs. Every organization is populated with these subgroups; sometimes they are nothing more than a friendship between as few as two people. The vast majority of these alliances do no harm to the organization; in fact they perform a valuable service in that they help meet the affiliation needs of its people.

Often, however, alliances are formed for negative reasons. People are disgruntled and find solace and comfort in relationships with people who share the same frustrations and the same complaints. At times, even negative alliances can provide a beneficial service for an organization in that they facilitate a catharsis of sorts. More often, however, they tend to work at cross purposes with the organization and they become pockets of resistance and insurrection; some evolve into major subcultures.

Negative subcultures are cancerous. If the organization's immune systems are not successful in keeping them in check, they begin to sap the strength and positive energy of the organization and diminish its ability to achieve its mission. Subcultures that do the most harm are congregations of losers that, conceptually, are not unlike a band of outlaws or street gangs.

The people who gravitate to these groups have not had winning experiences and have become, or are in danger of becoming, outcasts. Here, in the bosom of their subculture, they are not outcasts but find acceptance and support for their non-conformance. They have their own mission and moral code quite apart from and frequently at odds with the mission and values of the organization. After a time, groups of this type gain a legitimacy that enables them to compete effectively for the allegiance of the people. Which people? Typically those who are new and especially those whose performance might be classified as subpar are most attracted by these groups. These powerful subcultures are prevalent in many business organizations and significantly diminish productivity.

The best way to eliminate the competition of such sub-cultures is to prevent them from developing in the first place. As difficult a task as this may be it is far easier than breaking them up, once established.

The only way to prevent these bands of outcasts from forming is to work diligently to meet the needs of the people in your organization through its formal structure. You do so by insuring that people are given opportunities to affiliate with their peers and insuring that they are given opportunities to vent their frustrations and grievances. Every individual experiences frustration and everyone will have complaints. In the military it is said that it is "a soldier's right to complain." Complaints are natural occurrences and leadership needs to account for their impact every bit as much as an engineer must account for physical stresses in the design of a machine or structure.

As we have said, so often, leadership is the key. Positive leaders engineer their organizations to take these negative forces into account and to turn them, recycle them if you will, into positive energy. These leaders find meaningful forums in which people can voice their complaints (suggestion boxes by themselves do not fill the bill) and they respond to them with positive attention and meaningful action when issues are legitimate.

This has a dramatic, positive impact on people. A soldier's complaints are nothing more than gripes and the soldier clings to no illusions that anyone will listen or that any changes will be forthcoming as a result of his or her complaint. Organizations that are responsive to suggestions and grievances, with leaders who take action to resolve legitimate complaints or to implement positive suggestions, send a different message. Such organizations retard the development of negative subcultures because their people feel like winners through their participation. They know that they can make a difference and that they possess an element of power over their own destiny. Like a healthy self esteem, healthy organizations are those in which people believe they have a real ability to exert control over the outcomes in their workplace whether those outcomes are in higher quality products and services, better performance reviews, pay increases, or promotions.

Negative subcultures are almost always a haven for losers, for people who have not learned how to succeed in the mainstream. As difficult as it may seem, these men and women can be rehabilitated. The most effective way to approach existing subcultures is to seek ways to re-channel their energy. Find some issue that concerns the people in that subculture and challenge or sanction them to find a solution. Support them as much as you can without interfering with the process. What you are attempting is a transformation. You are teaching people how to break out of their loser's mentality and become winners. To do so takes great courage and a significant commitment of leadership for there are risks involved. The rewards of success are great, however, and can turn an entire organization around.

Winning one time will not be the end of the process. The first "win" is only the beginning. After the first win is briefly but joyfully celebrated, have a second challenge ready for them and follow that up with a stream of subsequent challenges. With every win comes an elevation of confidence on the part of the participants. Before long the transformation will be complete and those people, who were once outcasts, have become heroes and they possess an entirely new attitude about the organization.

The axiom that "the child who is hardest to love is the one that needs it the most," applies also to organizations. All people in the organization need positive attention from leadership and the people who are most difficult, need it the most.

## UNDERSTANDING ORGANIZATIONS AT THE MICRO LEVEL

Of all of the leadership challenges that this author has faced in a long career, the one that I recall with regret was the one where I failed to gain an adequate level of technical expertise with respect to the actual products and services we provided to our customers. I draw some solace from the knowledge that I did create value for my organization but I did not provide the level of leadership that it needed the most.

Positive leaders must have an intimate and detailed knowledge of the products and services that their organizations produce. They must be experts on every aspect of the production process that generates the end products and services and they must have a comparable level of technical knowledge of their company's supply chain partners. There is no excuse for failing to gain this level of expertise and not doing so is the result of nothing other than a commitment of insufficient strength.

We spoke earlier that it is much easier to learn the technical aspects of a job than it is to learn the principles of positive leadership. To be a positive leader, you must be able to put your personality on the line, each and every day. To gain the appropriate level of technical expertise requires only a relentless commitment to become of student of one's industry. Only then will a leader possess a sufficient knowledge and understanding of the products and the production process to insure that his or her people have the optimal resources and support necessary to lead the industry. Only then will a leader have a sufficient understanding of the industry to anticipate important changes in customer and supplier requirements and expectations while also recognizing new opportunities.

**Leadership Recruitment**

We must rethink the criteria by which we base our selection of candidates for promotion to supervisory positions. We must also reconsider our expectations of the leaders of our organizations.

The manner in which the current system works is that we reward outstanding performance by promoting people into management. This way we can be certain of keeping quality people and we can justify paying them a little more than their less productive colleagues. The result is that many people, probably a majority of those promoted, are advanced because they have good technical skills and work ethic. We assume that, with a training program now and then, they will acquire some leadership skills along the way.

Frequently, these individual discover that they are not happy with their new responsibilities and do not really understand what is required of them. If they were truthful, many would prefer to go back to their old job but that means giving up the additional money and prestige. More importantly, going backward looks like failure. So, these new supervisors and managers say nothing. They knuckle down and do the best job of which they are capable. Many also become unhappy, cynical, and mediocre supervisors who spend most of their energy trying to find a way to play the avoidance/bureaucracy game. One of the biggest challenges for technical champions who are asked to transition to a leadership role is that they have always been committed to being the best, technically, at what they do. In their new leadership role the demand has changed. They are now responsible for teaching their former colleagues to replace themselves as the technical champion of the company. They are now charged with teaching rather than doing.

This dilemma is commonly experienced in the overwhelming majority of companies that are, as a consequence, poorly led and largely ineffective operations.

We must dramatically alter the way we utilize the skills of our key people as well as the manner in which they are compensated. People who have outstanding technical skills but do not demonstrate effective leadership skills should be given the opportunity to remain in technical positions but still receive advanced compensation.

Individuals with good leadership skills, even if their technical capabilities are average, should be groomed for supervisory opportunities. This is a role he or she can play well and is also a role in which they can make a positive contribution to the success of the enterprise.

This is one area where the military may have something to offer as a model. With enlisted personnel above the rank of Private First Class (E-3), the United States Army splits its rank structure between non-commissioned officers—corporals (E-4) through Sergeant Major (E-9)—and Specialists also ranging upward from the E-4 pay grade. Non commissioned officers have command responsibilities while Specialists are advanced to comparable pay grades on the basis of their demonstrated technical performance and competency.

What we are striving for is a structure where men and women have opportunities to advance on the basis of where they can best bring value to his or her organization. Why would it not be in the best interest of business organizations to reward people on the basis of their contributions rather than on the basis of an artificial hierarchy? Why would it not be in the best interest of companies to reward individual contributions only in terms of the value he or she brings to the group? People with outstanding technical skills but mediocre leadership ability can best serve their employer and themselves by remaining in technical roles. Men and women who demonstrate exceptional leadership skills, irrespective of their technical competence, can best serve the interest of all parties through the exercise of their leadership. As we noted in the last section, however, moving into a leadership role does not obviate the need to continue to develop technical expertise. Leaders must be expected to make a commitment to become students of both spheres of influence.

Clearly, it is a fallacy to suggest that supervisors and managers should be paid more than their colleagues, simply because they are in positions of leadership. The value to the organization, as determined by recognizable criteria, should be the only basis for differentiating employees on the basis of compensation. Ultimately, people in positions of leadership with exceptional talent will have a more wide-ranged impact on the organization because their contributions transcend departmental boundaries and their compensation will rise accordingly. Until that happens, the value of their contributions may or may not be greater than that of their most skilled technician. Most companies do a good job of rewarding leaders, sometimes inappropriately so. Many of these same companies fall short in appropriately rewarding people for their technical competency and productivity. All it takes is to create an accelerated compensation path along which our technical champions can progress.

Placing more emphasis on the performance of the team as a whole will also enable companies to maximize the payback gleaned from their compensations systems. Teamwork creates real advantages in improving productivity, creativity, and distributing leadership responsibility. Team members, even without supervisory authority, not only have real opportunities to confront and resolve performance issues of other team members, they are motivated to do so when a teammate's performance may adversely affect their own compensation and incentives.

It seems clear to me that one of the root causes of declining productivity in the American economic theater is an archaic and dysfunctional compensation philosophy which often ignores performance, the only thing that truly matters. Far too many management staff earn disproportionately high pay relative to the achievement of their units. If that money were yanked away from undeserving management staff and distributed to all members of units with high quality and productivity, it would send an unequivocal message to the entire enterprise.

This is, in fact, one of the predominant criticisms leveled at American corporate leaders by their counterparts in Japan and Europe. That American chief executive officers, many of whom are the recipients of extraordinary levels of compensation while their companies are losing money and/or market share, is unjust and intolerable. Some have described American corporate CEOs as the new royalty rewarded more for the prestige of their offices than for their contributions to the success of their company. We need to see the pendulum begin to swing back from what is clearly a dysfunctional extreme.

Leadership requires an exemplary level of ethical commitment because the temptations of outrageous compensation are detrimental to not only the best interests of their company but also for the leader's own long-term best interests. Organizations must recruit and promote people into supervisory and management positions who demonstrate a flair for positive leadership for this is an indispensable component of business success. But recruitment and promotion is only the beginning. Organizations must demonstrate a relentless commitment to leadership training and development for very few great leaders are born to the role. For most, it is learned behavior of the most sophisticated kind and there is no end to the need for more wisdom and knowledge of the craft. Leadership is the heart and soul that drives organizations toward its mission and we do not devote sufficient energy and resources to the learning process.

The observations of one organization provide a classic example of the impact of powerful positive leadership. In this social service agency there were two divisions, each charged with different aspects of the service provided by the agency. Each division was comprised of a team of professionals and their unit supervisor.

The department was led by an Executive Director with a high level of commitment to the organization's mission and an equally significant presence in the community. The Executive Director's leadership style was somewhat reactive in that he could be both autocratic and participatory according to the needs of the situation. If his staff were content to be directed, he would direct. If they demanded freedom and responsibility he would adjust his approach to one of facilitation.

Of interest to us in our discussion of leadership are the dramatic differences in the personalities and approaches of the two divisions. One unit was characterized by:

- High morale
- Innovation
- High productivity

- A willingness to put in substantial amounts of uncompensated overtime
- Minimal complaints on the part of the staff
- A commitment to bureaucracy bashing, and
- A high esprit de corps

The second unit had:
- Low morale
- A never-ending flow of complaints on the part of the team that they were:
  - Unappreciated
  - Were not respected
  - Were the stepchild of the agency
- A dependence on the procedure manual
- A rigid bureaucratic structure

What accounted for the differences? Could it have been that the first group had the most talented people? The latter was unlikely, in this instance, as people were routinely rotated with a new employee starting in one unit and would subsequently be rotated to the other after a year or two.

The difference seemed almost totally the result of the leadership styles of the two supervisors. Both supervisors possessed a high level of commitment to the agency's mission and both were hard working professionals. The supervisor of the first division, however, was aggressive, demanding and had high expectations for his staff and, he encouraged risk-taking. He allowed his people a great deal of freedom and encouraged innovation. At the same time he was quick to respond to what he judged to be less than acceptable performance. Team play was the rule of the day and other rules were few and loose.

The second supervisor was far more personable and well-liked than her counterpart but played things much more conservatively. She encouraged few risks, played by a strict set of rules, and required staff to get approval before taking significant action. This latter supervisor spent most of her time at her desk doing paperwork while the former spent the majority of his time interacting with his staff, talking about cases with which they were involved.

The difference, of course, was that the first supervisor was a leader. The second was a bureaucrat. There is no question that the second unit made fewer mistakes and appeared less chaotic but in the things that really count, performance, it always fell short. The first supervisor was far from perfect. He was young and relatively inexperienced and was not nearly as positive as he thought himself to be. But, still, he was a leader more than just a supervisor. He had enthusiasm and a willingness to share that enthusiasm just as he demonstrated a willingness to share credit.

Time and again we see managers with good communication skills and only average technical skills out-perform their more skilled colleagues. The less effective supervisors do not seem to understand what leadership is all about and do not seem to know how to enlist the full participation of their people. Inspired leadership, even when flawed, almost always outperforms straight-laced management.

An organization is only as good as its leadership. The leadership challenge is to make something new and better. It is what the organization really needs, even if the organization does not realize the fact. Many managers do not understand the real needs of their organization and often erect barriers and obstacles by the score. Positive leaders may be more demanding than their colleagues but, when you succeed, they will pat you on the back, call you a hero, and then challenge you all over again.

Effective, positive leaders must guard against complacency and the powerful urge to back off when we get our operation working to the point that everyone seems reasonably satisfied with the outcomes they are creating. The reality is that the challenges never abate. The demands never end, the thing is never done, and no system is ever "just right," let alone perfect. Good leaders understand that organizations are fluid, living organisms and they look continuously for ways to improve their product, service, system, operation, or organization. Positive leaders understand that the point at which an idea, product, service, or process can no longer be improved is the precise moment in time that it becomes obsolete. Positive leaders incessantly implement small changes which sometimes seem insignificant. These small adjustments, viewed over a period of time, and grouped together, represent significant change.

These adjustments are analogous to the erosion of land by wind and water. Measured by the day or year the changes may not even be recognizable, but measured by the millennium and they result in a total reshaping of the Earth's surface. Change is ubiquitous. The process is virtually infinite. As a leader, your challenge is to build your organization to be as fully adaptive to the process of change as possible. Never is there an occasion to be complacent, lest you become stagnant. But people, it seems, are inclined to freeze the moment and preserve the status quo. How do we overcome these tendencies and keep our organization continuously at the crest of the wave?

Is there ever a time when there is too much change or when change, itself, is bad? The answer to this very perceptive question is that it all depends. Looking for ways to improve a process in order to create better outcomes is never bad unless the process is so disruptive that the change process obscures one's mission and purpose. Another case in which too much change is bad thing is when we keep changing our mission, purpose, goals, and objectives; in other words, when we keep moving the target. This type of change can be destructive. It is one thing to keep elevating our goals and objectives; it is quite another to keep replacing them with new and sometimes unrecognizable targets.

Leadership must work to maintain the momentum of change and keep people motivated and excited about the challenges facing the organization. We do not suggest that positive leaders never stop to look back at their organization's accomplishments or take time to celebrate their victories. In fact, they do these things often. These lookbacks and celebrations help create the focus on the organization's objectives because victories fuel the flame of desire for new victories.

The work environment should, as much as is possible, mirror life. A new day always brings something new and exciting to people who are enthusiastic about life. Every new day is a new opportunity for achievement, for winning. If people are enthusiastic about their jobs and about their company and its mission then they will begin to embrace change as the marvelous freedom from monotony that it is. Creating this culture within your organization is the type of challenge that only positive leaders can master.

We often make the mistake of examining other organizations and evaluating their successes in contrast to the shortcomings of our own. There is a tendency to conclude that the differences are the result of good luck or due to some other set of circumstances which are beyond our control. The truth is that although there may be some large environmental factors at work, and although luck does sometimes play a part, for the most part the difference between successful organizations and their not-so-successful counterparts is the result of thousands of little things over which positive leaders have complete control.

It is the leader's intimate knowledge of the organization that distinguishes the positive leader from a manager. The outcome of the leader's application of this knowledge is a vibrant, productive, winning organization that will inevitably become the benchmark of the industry.

## *six*

# COMMITMENT TO MISSION, VISION, AND VALUES

*"Courage is rightly considered the foremost of the virtues for upon it all others depend."*
— *Winston Churchill*

Commitment to Mission
Commitment to Values
Commitment to People
Commitment to Self & Self-Discipline
Commitment to Action
Commitment to Excellence

Without the commitment to convert dreams to plans, to action; dreams remain nothing more than a fantasy. Commitment is the active ingredient or agent that powers success. The fundamental component of commitment is the Positive Principle that begins with the unwavering belief that anything is possible and the unswerving faith that the individual man or woman is greater than the natural events taking place around him or her.

Commitment is such an integral part of positive leadership that it will emerge routinely throughout this work. Commitment is crucial to a positive self-esteem; it is a key element in the process of success; it powers organizations; and, it is a cornerstone to the process of motivating people.

So vital is commitment to our purpose that we have given it star billing. Commitment is the energy that fuels the system. We will talk about commitment from the macro perspective as well as from the micro. On the one hand it is commitment to a broad purpose and value system that lays the foundation for achievement. On the other, it is commitment that gives us the self-discipline to see objectives through to completion. Commitment is the essence of greatness and it gives us tremendous power to make things happen and to influence people.

- It is the <u>demonstrable</u> commitment to a mission, on the part of a leader, and to his or her vision of the future that rallies people to a cause and convinces them that the challenge is worthwhile and achievable.

- The secret to instilling values in people is a leader or parent's <u>demonstrable</u> commitment to a set of values.

- It is a leader's <u>demonstrable</u> commitment to his or her people that builds trust and loyalty in groups and organizations.

- It is the leader's <u>demonstrable</u> commitment to self and self-discipline that fosters the development of a positive esteem and self-discipline in others.

- It is the leader's <u>demonstrable</u> commitment to action that makes things happen, creates change, and creates opportunities for growth and learning. It is this same commitment to action that empowers people and organizations and that demystifies mistakes.

- It is a leader's <u>demonstrable</u> commitment to a standard of performance that elicits consistent achievement of performance goals on the part of his or her people. It is this commitment, more than anything the leader says, that drives excellence.

It is virtually impossible to attain any of these things without a clearly recognizable and consistent commitment to them on the part of leadership. Talk is not enough, as words and phrases, no matter how eloquent, are, in the final analysis, judged in the context of the leader's actions and behavior. The operative word is <u>demonstrable</u>.

As we will discuss in a later section, commitment is the driving force of motivation. When an individual has a deep-seated belief in a "thing," when he or she becomes convinced of the "thing's" possibility, when a plan of action is revealed that can make the "thing" a reality; people will make a commitment to it—they will declare their allegiance to it. They will then have a level of motivation that can sustain them through the process of making the "thing" happen.

The depth of the motivation is a function of the strength of the commitment. History offers many examples to illustrate that commitment can be strong enough to overcome obstacles of unimaginable size and complexity. The greater the commitment, the more powerful will be its force. Commitment is rooted in the deep-seated emotional well-spring of the individual or group.

Passion is a vital component of commitment and few successes can happen without it. What do we mean by passion? That you feel strongly about your mission, your goals and objectives, and about the values that drive them.

Look back through the history of any civilization and the one characteristic that personifies the most powerful leaders is that they believed with zeal, leaving little or no doubt among their following as to the depth of their passion.

Rule number one for leaders is to believe passionately in your cause and rule number two is to communicate those beliefs at every opportunity. Every time you address your people in whole or in part, sell your mission, share your vision of the company or organization's future, and demonstrate the values of the organization in everything that you do and say. Every time you walk through the plant, sell your mission and share your vision and values. Every time you have a one-to-one conversation with your people, sell your mission and share your vision and values. Every time you talk to your children, share your vision and your values and tell them how important they are.

It is a simple but effective rule of thumb that if your people do not know exactly what you are going to say, you do not say it with sufficient regularity. Do not worry about being redundant, because redundancy cannot hurt your organization when it comes to espousing the values that drive it. It is damaging, however, when people do not know what is important to your organization. If your people cannot recite the company's mission when called upon to do so, then you are not doing your job. So important is one's understanding of the mission and purpose of an organization that it is routine for inspectors of a quality system's certification authority to ask people throughout an organization to state their company's mission statement during the certification process.

A good parent hugs their children and tells them they are loved every day and it is this ongoing reinforcement that builds confidence and character. Children do not want you to stop just because you told them you loved them the day before and the day before that. Even when they become teenagers and are embarrassed if you hug them in public, they still need it in private.

Your employees require the same daily vigilance. The message is never redundant. There is an axiom in advertising that, just about the time people are beginning to sicken at the sight of your ad, is when it begins to influence their buying decisions.

When we begin to lose sight of our mission, we begin to make decisions that are counter-productive, that serve secondary rather than primary agendas. Focus on your mission keeps you on course.

I am a passionate baseball fan. I love to watch baseball and coach baseball and when I was young I loved to play the game. Some of my most memorable lessons about positive leadership were learned while coaching Little League.

One season, during the all-star tournament, I observed another coach handle a situation so badly that it made an indelible impression and seemed to justify the negative reputation that youth leagues have garnered in recent years. This coach's team was trailing by a run in the last inning and the winning runs were on base with two outs. At bat was the team's best hitter. I was scouting and standing at the end of the dugout where I could hear every word.

The coach called the boy over, a strapping twelve-year old, and said, "We need you buddy! It's all up to you! Don't let us down; the whole team is counting on you!"

The young man walked to the plate full of determination and proceeded to pop up to end the game—an exciting victory for the other team. The batter walked back to the dugout with his head hanging. The coach put his arm around him and said, "Forget it! You did your best."

But, of course, it was too late. The boy had carried the burden of success or failure for his team and he had let them down. In his mind, he was a failure and a loser. All I could do was shake my head. Maybe Little League deserves a bad reputation, I thought to myself. Little did I know that just one night later, I would face a similar situation.

My team played the next evening and we went into the bottom of the last inning trailing by two runs. Our best hitter was due at the plate. There were two outs and the bases were loaded. In my mind I'm thinking, "We need you buddy! It's all up to you! Don't let us down; the whole team is counting on you."

Fortunately, I heard myself and realized what I was thinking and I am so thankful that I had an opportunity to learn from a colleague's mistake. When I called the boy over my approach was totally different from what I had heard twenty-four hours earlier.

I said, "This is the at bat you've dreamt about for as long as you can remember, so listen closely. I want you to relax and take a deep breath! Now, go out there and enjoy this moment. Give it your best effort and whatever happens, I'm proud of you."

My story has a different ending, as well. The young boy responded with a grand slam home run for a dramatic win—the kind of which dreams are made.

Did my advice make a difference? You may draw your own conclusions but I believe it did. It helped the child approach the situation as an opportunity to live out a dream. It was an opportunity to succeed through the use of his talents and abilities rather than as a burden or as an opportunity to fail. When we have no fear of failure we are able to maximize our talents.

The most important lesson has to do with one's focus on one's mission. I realized that my mission was not to win Little League baseball games but to provide young boys and girls with an opportunity to learn to play the game of baseball; to experience the thrill of competition, the value of teamwork; and, to develop their athletic potential. My objective was to teach them to give their best effort without fear of failure. The particular game in my story was a young boy's "one moment in time" and, as his coach, I was only an instrument.

My counterpart had been focused on his own desire to win; on his own needs. He viewed the child as an instrument of his own objectives or at least that is what we must surmise from his actions.

The lesson to positive leaders is to understand and be committed to your mission. Focus on the correct mission is the penultimate key to long-term success. Judge every action on the basis of how effectively it serves the mission. Periodically, remind yourself what the mission is, as it is easy to drift off course. Remind your people, relentlessly. Yes, it is nice to win but like making money, winning games is what happens when you do things right over the long haul. Many people experience short-term victory without achieving long-term success (win the battle but lose the war). Positive leaders are successful over the long term and, in the process, are frequently victorious.

Never, ever sacrifice your mission for a short-term objective.

Commitment and passion are neutral forces, however, and in the hands of someone with a warped sense of values they can do great harm. An example from one of history's darkest periods serves to illustrate how powerful leadership of one committed individual forever changed the face of the world. Even though it illustrates the power of "the dark side of the force" it teaches a lesson.

Once again Adolph Hitler illustrates our point. Hitler, we now know, was a deranged man but he was a phenomenally powerful leader. He was fanatical in his belief that his people, the German people—the Aryan race—were destined to rule the world. So powerful was his belief, so strong was his passion that he was willing to do anything to enhance the power of his message and he committed all of his human energy to the fulfillment of this one mission.

It was a commitment at an emotional level and he appealed to the rawest of emotions of the German people. It was a time in history when the German people were desperate for Hitler's message of hope. There is ample evidence to show that individuals were often appalled by his methods and by his unabashed willingness to resort to force but they were a people whose "national self esteem" had been devastated and they hungered for a cause to embrace.

The German people were not unlike the poor man who finds it easy to overlook the moral/social code which says it is wrong to steal. All he knows is that his children are starving and there sits a loaf of bread, his for the taking. If the hunger is sufficiently powerful, he will take the bread and will find it easy to rationalize the action in his mind. By the time he observes his children devouring his booty he will have convinced himself that he did the right thing, morally and ethically.

It is a seduction of sorts. Once one has rationalized one's behavior there are few moral impediments to stop him the next time he is faced with the opportunity to steal. In fact, he is almost compelled to steal again. The act, repeated, serves to reinforce the rationalization. The amazing thing is that, when hunger is great enough, the individual remains the moral man he was from the beginning and his core values remain surprisingly unchanged. The man knows it is wrong to steal but he also knows it is immoral to watch his children starve.

It is a real life example of Leon Festinger's "cognitive dissonance theory." Another man who steals the bread, without the strong need to feed a starving family, will also be quick to rationalize his behavior. He will do so by subtly adjusting his value system. One might expect to hear such justifications as "that baker has been price-gouging for years" or "that store will never miss it!" "They're too rich anyway!"

"Besides, it's just a big corporation; it is not like stealing from real people." Again, repetition reinforces correctness of the behavior and it gets easier and easier with each act, and gradually the behavior becomes habitualized.

This is similar to that which happened to the German people. In the case of the Nazis who actually carried out the persecution of the Jews and other non-Aryan minorities and who actually terrorized the political opposition, they quickly overcame whatever moral scruples they may have possessed at the outset and viewed their mission as morally right and just—as morally compelling. Undoubtedly, such moralization would have been necessary to maintain their sanity. In the case of the German people as a whole, the majority of whom took no direct, active part in the brutality of the Nazi regime; they had another moral choice.

Hitler's leadership brought significant improvement in the economic quality of life and to the national pride of the people. The choice of the average man or woman was simply between actively dissenting against the Nazi Party, at the risk of death or other physical harm or social and economic ruination or, turning their back on the brutality as an unfortunate but necessary means to an end. No doubt they hoped it to be a temporary aberration.

It is easy for men and women today to criticize the German people of fifty years ago because we do not really understand the extraordinary courage it takes to stand up to an organized, politically legitimate mob of thugs.

How many Americans get involved in the defense of an innocent victim of a crime on the streets of our cities and neighborhoods? How many will even come forth to testify against the perpetrators of such acts? How many Americans will speak up in protest at a social event when your neighbors or acquaintances display their racism and spout off against blacks and other minorities? Sadly, the answer to all of these questions is that very few of us have the courage to do anything at all, so what makes us think that we would have acted differently than the average Berliner of the Thirties and Forties, or that what happened in Nazi Germany could not happen right here in the United States of America?

What is the point of this discussion? It is that leaders who are totally, even fanatically committed to their values can have a phenomenal impact on the people around them. If the value systems of those leaders are corrupt it can do great harm. If leaders come forth who are equally committed to positive values they can do enormous good.

Positive leadership teaches us to use the great power of commitment to accomplish good things. Positive leaders function on a foundation of core values that are positive and life-affirming. It is the positive leader's unfaltering commitment to these positive values that distinguishes them from users and abusers of people.

**Faith**

Faith is the medium through which positive power flows. Many businessmen and women, it seems, are troubled that a number of motivational writers and speakers come from and espouse a conservative Christian, sometimes fundamentalist background. These men and women tend to reject the concepts put forth by these authors on the grounds that it is religious "mumbo jumbo."

This is a tragic mistake! One can draw upon the powers of positive thinking and positive leadership, and through these powers achieve much success in one's life, no matter in what kind of "higher good" one believes.

In truth, the vast majority of us believe in something greater than ourselves. We may define and describe it differently but it's there. We may shout those beliefs from the hilltops or we may speak of it only rarely, considering it a private and personal thing. Some of us may not even understand it but the reality of our belief is part of us and affects the way we live our lives on a daily basis.

So, whoever you are and however you define it, place your faith in that which you believe. Having a real and deeply rooted faith can create great peace of mind and opens up many channels of opportunity.

With such faith, life can be truly beautiful and bountiful no matter what blessings and tragedies may befall us.

Why is so much emphasis placed on faith?

Faith cannot and will not make the world a perfect place or protect one from life's natural course of events. Life is full of joy and tragedy, hot and cold, day and night, rich and poor, and life and death. Faith gives one the strength to accept and make the best of life's vicissitudes. It allows one to hold onto the fundamental truth that an individual's value, freedom, and dignity cannot be diminished by mere worldly events.

Faith cannot insure that all of your decisions will be good decisions, free from the risk of natural consequences. Faith can, however, assure that all decisions, whatever their consequences, will result in learning and growth and that each will contribute to the long-term enrichment of our life.

Faith cannot insure that all ventures will be successful and many will surely fail. Faith enables the individual to profit from all experiences, both successes and failures. Most crucially, faith will insure a successful life as measured by a much greater benchmark than dollars and cents.

In J. D. Salinger's *Franny and Zooey*, Zooey tells his sister that their eldest, and now deceased, brother Seymour once told him to shine his shoes prior to appearing on their radio program. When Zooey protested that no one would know, Seymour told him to do it for the "fat lady." Zooey pictured a fat lady out there, somewhere, sitting on her porch in a rocking chair, listening to his radio broadcast. Franny replied that she, too, remembered Seymour's "fat lady."

Franny and Zooey came to believe that Seymour's "fat lady" was the symbolic representation of Jesus Christ. This message suggests that, whether we are artists or laborers, we should strive to give our best, not just for the gratification of our own ego, but for the good that is in man and in the world. It is another way of saying that an honest job, done well, through the absolute best efforts of the doer, adds an element of beauty and good to the world. It is commitment to this ideal that is inherent in positive leadership—that there is virtue in a job done to the best of one's ability; that such efforts enrich our lives and the lives of the people with whom we interact.

When moments of despair set in, one can feel the cancer of self-doubt creep in and begin to spread throughout one's consciousness. It is at these times that most people back off from challenges and turn their backs on opportunity. They rationalize their behavior with such assertions as "Well, it was just a pipe dream!" or "I'm happier just being average!" or "I'm happier blending in."

Often, the only thing that distinguishes a successful businessperson from an average worker is confidence, courage, and commitment, all of which are rooted in a man or woman's faith.

**Micro Level**

At the micro level, commitment is the thing that distinguishes winners from losers and champions from the rest of the field. The world of athletics is full of wonderful examples of individuals whose dedication to a goal; whose willingness to make sacrifices; whose self-discipline to a practice regimen; whose determination to overcome obstacles and to come back from defeat have resulted in extraordinary achievements. Hall of Fame baseball player, Nolan Ryan pitched his seventh no-hitter at the age of forty-four. It remains an unprecedented achievement as the result of a tremendous talent, but much more than just talent. There have been many great pitchers in the game of baseball but Nolan Ryan is the only one to pitch seven no-hitters, in fact no one else has pitched more than four. No pitcher has been so dominant at such an advanced age for competitive athletics. What separates Nolan Ryan from the pack, in addition to his incredible gifts? His commitment! He worked hard to master his craft. He worked every day on a demanding regimen of weights and conditioning. Even pitching a no-hitter earned no days off as Nolan Ryan often celebrated his accomplishment in the training room, preparing for his next start.

Denny Doyle, former major league ballplayer and founder of the Doyle Baseball School, tells a story about newly inducted Hall of Famer, Wade Boggs. During a portion of his career and his time with the Boston

Red Sox, Wade Boggs was acknowledged as the best hitter in baseball. During one of his greatest seasons, the Red Sox had an unexpected day off due to torrential rains. Rather than taking the day off, Boggs, who was batting over .400 at the time, was seen coming out of the dugout, with bat and tee in hand. In the driving rain he trotted out to the sheltered hitting area in the outfield. There he took his routine 150 swings.

Many individuals at Wade Boggs' level of success might say they didn't need to practice. Others recognize that they excel because of a disciplined practice regimen. In anything we do, our success will be determined by our level of commitment and our commitment is measured by the effort we put into the venture, by our work ethic. Champions practice their craft, they develop a regimen that hones the skills critical to success, and they dedicate themselves to that regimen. We can think of a disciplined practice regimen as nothing more than an applied commitment.

The examples are everywhere, in athletics, in the performing arts, in academia, in science and research, and in business. Men and women who achieve at the highest level of excellence, whatever their endeavor or venue, reach a pinnacle and remain there through applied commitment.

The world is full of talented people but not all talented people are successful. Similarly, not all successful people are exceptionally talented. The distinguishing characteristic of successful people everywhere is the level of commitment with which they apply their individual talents. Just as not every major league pitcher can throw seven no-hitters, not every human being accomplish great things. We are, after all constrained by a finite and unequal amount of talent. What is important is that we strive for the highest level of achievement of which we are capable. Commitment is dedication, hard work, sacrifice, determination, and self-discipline all rolled into one.

**Hard Work**

Few people understand the meaning of hard work. They put in their thirty-five to forty hours per week and maybe tackle a few projects around the house but they measure their life by the amount of time they spend in leisure activities. During the week, these individuals live for the weekend and during the day they live for quitting time, one eye always focused on the clock.

If you ask these people, they will insist that they work hard. It is true that some lead a comfortable life without working hard but it is rare to excel at something without working hard in the truest sense of the word. Working hard means to devote one's energy to a project and to do so, fully. Working hard means to be absorbed with the task to the exclusion of time consciousness. Working hard can often mean long hours and even seven days a week.

The challenge for truly exceptional performers is learning how to invest themselves in their mission without sacrificing the other things that are important in life, with family the most obvious. Indeed, many successful people pay an enormous price with respect to the quality of their relationships with their spouse and children. What is the answer? The answer is balance or equilibrium. Just as freedom only works when balanced by responsibility, our commitments must also be balanced. Is this an easy thing to do, to excel at one's craft and also excel as a life-partner or parent? Of course not but neither is it impossible. What it requires is the same thing that excellence in any endeavor requires—commitment. The payoff is fulfillment.

For many people, fulfillment often feels unobtainable and the reason, simply, is that they do not understand that fulfillment is a consequence of action; it is one of the payoffs of hard work and commitment. Individuals who feel unfulfilled often go through life in the so-called, "middle class" groove and never experience real contentment and satisfaction with their lives. They yearn for something more, usually something quite unidentifiable to them, something that will fill the tremendous void they feel inside. Some never come to understand that the void in their life is the result of their lack of commitment to something in life, something that demands hard work of them; something that requires that they give fully of themselves.

That leisure is perceived as one of the most precious commodities, in our society is, I think, a symptom. Not solely a symptom of affluence but rather of men and women who have lost sight of what is important in life.

We have taken the art and craft—the sense of accomplishment (winning) out of the work we ask of people. Because a sense of accomplishment is one of the most gratifying things in life, its absence from our work-life has turned work into a necessary evil rather than as an opportunity for meaning and fulfillment. Not surprisingly then, many people view their work as something to be endured, to be set aside as quickly as possible so that maximum time can be devoted to other activities, activities deemed more important.

Positive leaders provide their people with opportunities to be creative, to develop their craft and to experience real accomplishment (winning). They bring the thrill and excitement back to the workplace, making it a place of challenges and adventures. The result—their people begin to derive satisfaction from their work. Work becomes meaningful. With each increase in the degree of satisfaction, the more meaningful their work becomes, the more willing people are to invest more of themselves. This is commitment.

With surprising speed, positive leaders have a fully committed team of people for whom work is a source of fun, pride, joy, and fulfillment. There are few challenges that fail to yield to a team of committed people.

We speak of motivation a great deal and it is vital that a business have a motivated workforce. Unfortunately, motivation is not something that leaders can instill in people. Motivation must come from within the individual and what leaders do is to nurture the motivation. As we will see in a later chapter, motivation springs from the well of commitment. Positive leaders work at building commitment, confident that motivation will take care of itself.

It is so easy for people to become complacent—to get comfortable with a life of minimal challenge—that inertia is one of the most difficult obstacles for people to overcome. If you want to accomplish something special you must be willing to make sacrifices for your goal—to make a commitment to it. The adage "no pain, no gain!" is not without truth. Many of us dream of doing something special with our lives but few are willing to do what it takes to accomplish that special something. It is far easier to stay in our comfort zone and wait for good fortune to arrive at our door.

Successful leadership in today's economic environment requires a major commitment. Positive leaders must work long and hard, but find it uplifting rather than an exhausting experience. It leaves one with a positive attitude, a happy outlook, and with plenty of energy to devote to family, other social relationships and commitments, and even to leisure.

Others are hooked on leisure time. They want to sit idly and watch television, tinker with hobbies, play games, compete in athletics—they want to enjoy the good things in life. For the most part, there is nothing wrong with these things and many positive leaders engage in these activities as well. The difference is that these activities make wonderful diversions but they are not the "stuff of life." None of these activities are as enjoyable or meaningful as the contributions of fully committed positive leaders and no leisure activities contribute as much to the welfare of the community. Yet, millions of Americans live their life as if these activities are the most important things in their life. They do as little as possible on the job so as to conserve energy for their leisure time. Others forego activities with their families, either spending huge chunks of time away from home playing or at home in front of the television.

When their employer gets in financial difficulty they wonder why. When they are faced with forced layoffs, they think it unfair. When their marriage turns sour they blame their spouse. When their children seem uninterested in them they blame an entire generation and when their community begins to deteriorate they blame society. Do these individuals accept any responsibility for the problems that confront them? Often not. They remain sad, disillusioned, unfulfilled and, ultimately, lonely people who never come to the realization that the quality of their life is a direct result of their own contributions, or lack thereof.

Committed people are givers and their commitment to giving of themselves makes the difference!

Aside from all that committed men and women can accomplish, positive leaders are happier and less stressed than other human beings. Yes, they face many challenges, many uncertainties, and they experience failure and disappointment far more often than the average person yet none of these things create stress or unhappiness. (They experience failure and disappointment more often because they extend themselves more often.) Stress is the emotional response people experience when they feel out of control; when they feel helpless and hopeless; and when they do not feel good about themselves relative to the task or challenge before them.

Positive leaders rarely experience these feelings because they understand that success is a process and not a destination, a process that naturally includes periods of difficulty, of ups and downs. Roller coasters have both ups and downs but the downs are just as exhilarating as the ups and, in fact, without both ups and downs the roller coaster would not be exhilarating at all.

Another analogy is that non-swimmers, or even poor swimmers, feel stress, often in the form of panic, when their mouth, nose, and eyes are under water. It is a frightening thing when you have no confidence that you will ever breathe again. Good swimmers, however, are trained to breathe in a rhythmic pattern that is synchronized with their stroke. For a significant portion of the time, they swim with their face under water yet it creates no stress, no fear, and no panic. To be under water is a natural part of the process for which they are well-trained, a process in which they have great confidence opportunities to breathe will occur at predictable intervals. It becomes an unconscious process so that the only feelings swimmers experience are exhilaration, fun, a sense of accomplishment, and the contented feeling that comes at the end of a healthy workout.

Positive leadership training provides the same unconscious response to the cycles of work in any challenging environment. Times of challenge, difficulty, unexpected problems, and even natural disasters are all part of a natural, cyclical process that is always followed by a breathing time when the body and spirit are refueled and refreshed by the breath of accomplishment and the thrill of victory.

Most of us tap only a small portion of our potential because of our failure to overcome inertia. We want the best out of life but we want it for little or no cost. Achievement does not come free of charge.

Two boys want to play on their high school's varsity baseball team but both have weaknesses that keep them from reaching their goal. One makes a commitment to that goal, lays out a plan of action that includes a regimen of working with weights and hitting off of a batting tee in a makeshift batting cage in his basement. He disciplines himself to this regimen for a requisite number of hours per week during the winter months prior to the start of the baseball season.

The other boy, of comparable natural ability, takes no such action but instead spends his winter dreaming about making the team. Come tryouts, both boys give it their best effort but only one can make the team. That one boy has positioned himself to succeed is so obvious that it doesn't need mentioning except that this is a story that repeats itself every day, in all aspects of life for many boys and girls, men and women.

Again, we look to professional sports for an analogy. A few athletes are so talented that success seems to come naturally and effortlessly. For most, success goes to those who work the hardest to develop their abilities. The world is full of gifted athletes who fail to make it in collegiate or professional sports, just as it is full of gifted people in other venues who fail to realize their potential.

The "hard work ethic" does not refer to just hard physical labor but to a willingness to work as hard as it takes to complete a difficult job, well.

Employers frequently complain that "young people don't want to work anymore!" and truly, many young people do not seem to know what it means to dedicate themselves to a job. Large numbers of people seem simply unwilling to work as hard as it takes and seem more and more willing to be satisfied with getting the job done as quickly as possible with as little effort as possible and with minimal concern with respect to the quality of their output.

We can argue long and hard about the causes of this phenomenon but the relevant question for present-day employers is, "What can we do about it?"

The challenge, then, is how can we train a workforce to be committed to quality effort, hard work, and pride of achievement? This is clearly the leadership challenge of our time and successes are occurring every day. Tom Peters and his colleagues, in their several publications (*In Search of Excellence, A Passion for Excellence,* and *Thriving on Chaos*), provide numerous examples of companies that are doing something differently and achieving real results for their effort.

The key is that leadership is also hard work and takes a full commitment. But it is not enough to be demanding and authoritative. We must be creative and imaginative and we must involve people at every opportunity.

**Integrity**

Integrity is nothing more than commitment to a set of values. One of the sad truths about our society is an apparently diminishing integrity. One of the many part-time jobs I have held was as a desk-clerk at a small motel. Our price for one person per room was $26.00 and $28.00 for two people. I was always amazed at the number of people who would lie to save $2.00 by registering as a single, instead of a twosome and then sneak the second person in. It seems like such a little thing but if $2.00 is all it takes for a person to sacrifice his or her integrity, can the individual be expected to be honest and reliable when the stakes are high? Our point is: if a person sells out for $2.00 he will sell out for any price and that a frighteningly large number of people in our society sell out for $2.00.

In my life as a trial court administrator, one of the judges for whom I worked delighted in shocking people who questioned his integrity by responding to the effect, "Yes, I can be bought! But so far, no one has come close to my price." It always seemed to be a bad joke to me. Whether there is a price at which all men and women will relinquish their integrity is a point that must be debated elsewhere. I would like to think that the price has nothing to do with integrity any more than stealing two dollars is different than stealing a million dollars. Both actions constitute theft.

The lack of non-negotiable integrity is, I submit, at the root of the problems of society and that much of what we see going on is a symptom of this absence of integrity.

In leadership, integrity means possessing high standards and adhering to them. Sometimes this means appearing to be unreasonable and it often means being unpopular. "What's the big deal? So he didn't do it exactly the way you expected. It was close."

One of the truly distinguishing characteristics of winning organizations is that their leaders expect nothing less than the best and, more importantly, <u>accept</u> nothing less than the best. Positive leaders are relentless in their pursuit of excellence.

There is a simple rule, "If you are not willing to give me your very best, save yourself the trouble and go work elsewhere. I tell you now and I will tell you later that I will accept nothing less. Close isn't good enough."

The moment you begin to make exceptions and lower your standards and expectations, you have lost the battle and the war. In fact, you no longer have standards and expectations that are meaningful because you have sacrificed your integrity. People quickly learn that what you say doesn't really mean what you say it does. The reality is always determined by your actions. You can talk at length about standards but if you deal with real situations by accepting less than you say you want, then the latter becomes the reality. People have learned not to take your words seriously. You no longer have credibility. Even positive leaders must sometimes live with outcomes that are less than what they wanted and find acceptable but, in the real world, sometimes we simply must move on to the next challenge. What distinguishes positive leaders is that the disappointing outcome does not result in lowered expectations. Positive leaders simply learn what there is to be learned from the disappointing outcome and strive more ardently to exceed expectations the next time around.

Remember when you evaluate people you are not looking for okay and average is not acceptable. You are looking for "A" work and "A" work is the only kind that will be found acceptable. You must be relentless in your pursuit. Remaining true to one's values is difficult. Many people want to be easy going. We want our people to do a good job but it seems to take and extraordinary effort to demand excellence all the time. Our people seem to let down a notch so frequently that it seems like all we do is nitpick at them. Yet positive leadership must be constant and unyielding and it takes great effort and commitment. How one accomplishes this is also important. There is no middle ground. This is exactly the effort required if you truly desire an outstanding organization.

Each time you turn your back or avert your eyes to marginal performance, you have sent a message that says "this level of performance is okay." What people conclude is "The boss may bitch and gripe once in a while but if we are persistent he/she will give in, we will wear him/her down."

It is much like disciplining your children; it is a battle of wills. The child will persist in their behavior until he is convinced that he cannot win. Any time the child outlasts the parent, her will to persist is reinforced and revitalized. It is imperative that parents and leaders be consistent and relentless in their pursuit of acceptable performance. Integrity is more than just being honest; it is also relentless commitment to values.

Does it ever end? Yes and no! There clearly is a point at which people begin to understand that the mission is not a game and that you are serious. Their will to dictate their own terms is overcome by your will to demand excellence and they begin to internalize your value system. At this point the job changes. It now becomes imperative to develop feedback and incentive/recognition systems that reward their achievement. Once this has been implemented you have pretty effectively won the war. The temptation at this point is to begin assuming that people no longer need the constant reminders. The reality is that the same "relentlessness" is always required.

People come and go and there will always be new personalities entering your organization for whom the process begins anew. The difference is that, now, the entire organization is involved in setting the example and it reinforces the expectations and standards that you outline for the new person. It is no longer just words, the newcomer can see the standards demonstrated and modeled for him/her throughout the organization.

If you occupy a position of leadership at any level of an organization you can carve out a territory of excellence. You must make an irrevocable commitment to it, however, and devote as much energy as necessary to make it happen. You are, in effect, the ignition system and ignition systems require a great deal of energy but once the engine has been started it generates its own power; inertia—positive inertia—takes over.

Managers are always looking for systems to install that will do this job for them. They want job descriptions and job-performance evaluations that will solve their problems for them. More often than not the people on the line or in the field will ask for job descriptions and job-performance evaluations. This is a sure sign that a leadership void exists.

Job descriptions and job-performance evaluation systems can be effective tools in some situations but they cannot solve any problems. Only people can solve problems. Whenever people cry out for job descriptions and performance evaluations, what they yearn for is leadership. They are telling you that no one is giving them two of the most important things one finds in effective, dynamic organizations: expectations (meaning mission with specific goals and objectives) and feedback.

So, they think, "if only we had a job description we wouldn't need leadership!" This sounds good, depending on one's perspective, but it never works. The truth is, if we had strong, positive leadership we wouldn't need job descriptions. There are no substitutes for leadership but that doesn't mean job descriptions cannot be useful. Job descriptions can be effective tools in the hands of positive leadership.

What job descriptions can do is improve communication and provide a higher degree of clarity. It is the communication that is important and job descriptions are only one way leaders can communicate expectations to their employees. In small organizations, they may add little if any value. As organizations grow larger and communication becomes more challenging, job descriptions often prove to be useful tools, provided they are easily adaptable to the frequent changes that occur in most business environments. We recommend the use of job matrices and an integrated performance management system. By integrated, we mean that we do not rely on evaluations a couple of times per year rather that supervisors and employees utilize the integrated performance management system for daily, ongoing feedback with respect to expectations and performance, outcomes and productivity.

Job descriptions are just one example of things that diminish in importance in the presence of strong, positive leadership. Rules and regulations are another example. There may be a few basic rules and regulations that are necessary to help organizations run effectively and efficiently but, as we pointed out in an early section of this book, many of the rules organizations create are necessary only when leadership fails to do its job. Many rules owe their existence to a leadership void.

In an ideal scenario, when a problem arises and an employee takes advantage of the freedom the employer grants to her employees, the supervisor or manager goes to the individual and addresses the issue face to face, in a frank discussion. Managers and supervisors who lack the confidence to deal with such issues face to face, often create a rule governing their employees' behavior with respect to the issue in question. Inevitably, such rules restrict the freedom of employees who routinely act responsibly while those that do not, expend energy figuring out a way to sidestep the rule. Rules also have a way of multiplying to the point that it becomes costly to administer them. The former approach, "we don't do that here!" requires only a commitment on the part of leadership to take action. As a result, problems are resolved quickly at the lowest possible level and rules are few in number. As we said earlier, it is the "few rules theory of leadership."

## No One is Perfect

Just how important is commitment and dedication to the mission? It is paramount! I once worked for a man who was a royal pain. He was pompous and egotistical and he could take credit for someone else's accomplishments in a blink of an eye. He would massage statistics to suit his purpose and he would often say whatever was needed to get something done, with minimal regard for the truth.

I used to wonder how this guy rose to prominence and why people were so impressed with him. I struggled to understand how he got away with the things he did and I could prepare lists of things he did wrong as a leader. It was not until several years after I left the organization that I began to understand this man and his success, given his apparent imperfections.

What was his secret? In one word – commitment! He was totally committed to the mission of his organization and he wore that commitment like a badge of honor, for the world to see. The sincerity of his dedication, coupled with the natural appeal of the message—the mission itself—won the support and cooperation of people in positions of power. Pure and simple this man was a powerful leader!

The man's idiosyncrasies—those little imperfections that drove me to distraction—become insignificant in light of real achievement. After all, which of us is perfect? To this day he remains one of my heroes. His dedication to his cause is as solid as the Earth and his accomplishments outweigh his imperfections. His example can teach us much. Being a powerful leader and being fully committed to one's mission can overcome man's imperfections as well as other obstacles.

**Doing It Right**

Many years ago, while undergoing medical corpsman training at Fort Sam Houston in San Antonio, I learned a valuable lesson in the importance of commitment. We were taught to give injections with a forceful jab of the needle into the living tissue of our fellow GIs' arms. The successful poke, if you will, was done quickly and decisively, causing little if any discomfort, much to our relief and surprise. Most importantly, the medication (the mission) could then be injected, enabling prompt absorption by the patient's body with minimal tissue damage.

Success resulted from careful observation of these facts:

1. If done properly, pain or tissue damage was minimal and that which did occur would result only from:
    b. Burning or irritation caused by the medication itself—an occurrence that is unavoidable
    c. Accidental puncture of nerve tissue—an occurrence controlled only by pure chance and that is largely improbable. (Since it cannot be prevented one need not worry about it.)
2. Knowledge that the pain that does occur is miniscule when weighed against the benefits of the medication
3. Confidence that the needle is sufficiently sharp to perform effectively and painlessly, when properly utilized, and
4. Confidence that we have the physical skill and capability to insert the needle effectively (quickly and decisively.)

Thus we are presented with a totally achievable task, one that is performed successfully by thousands of professional health-care workers, daily.

In spite of the relative simplicity of the task, there were numerous trainees who found the task painfully difficult to accomplish. They would, for example, place the point of the needle on a patient's skin and then push, twist, and grind it; or, worse yet, would get it halfway in, then lose faith and withdraw, then try again. You can imagine the pain of the experience. On one occasion, I actually observed an incident where both the GIs, one on either side of the needle, fainted simultaneously.

What is even more frightening is that there is a percentage of the population of health-care professionals who daily subject their patients to their pointedly inadequate skill and seem oblivious to it all.

What contributes to this inability to perform such a simple but important task? Four things:

- Ignorance
- Fear

- Lack of focus
- Willful misconduct

Ignorance, fear, and lack of focus can be remediated through the commitment of the positive leader. If the last of these is the culprit, then get the person out of your organization. There is no room in any organization for people who flagrantly violate the spirit of the mission yet, time and again, leaders turn their back on such behavior because they are afraid or, because they do not know how to combat it. This is one of the most common causes of low trust in an organization, because nothing spawns social apathy more quickly than leaders who will not stand up for that which is right; leaders who fail to demonstrate their commitment!

**Innovation**

Occasionally innovations that revolutionize the world happen by accident but this is rare. Leaders who wait for such accidents to occur rarely achieve great things.

Most innovations happen as a result of repeated experimentation, through the process of trial and error. Often, innovations are spawned by the knowledge gleaned from a mistake or, more often than not, a series of mistakes or failures.

When we take aim at a target for the very first time, rarely do we hit the mark. Instead, we analyze the results of our effort and make adjustments to bring us closer to the mark. In most instances, it takes a number of attempts and subsequent adjustments before we are successful. Even then, our job is not complete because attaining our objective once does not insure that future efforts will succeed. No archer hits the bull's eye one hundred percent of the time. The archer practices his or her craft continuously, making incessant microscopic changes and adjustments to increase the quality of the effort, but never is perfection attained. Perfection may be approached but it remains ever elusive.

Life in the business world is much the same and there is no place for complacency. The key ingredient to success is continuous innovation and improvement in product quality and unwavering search for new market opportunities. In the latter case, it is listening to customers to uncover unmet needs that are within the capability of the business. Businesses that fail to innovate, fail to keep up. They fail, plain and simple. Some hold on longer than others but the end result is as inevitable as death to living organisms.

The unceasing challenge is to reach, to strive, to try, to experiment, and to seek out ideas with dogged persistence from every conceivable source and from every individual who may possibly know anything about your business. The more people who are involved in this process the more likely you are to find a marketable idea. It is truly a numbers game far more than it is won by genius. When genius does exist it generally manifests itself through reaching, striving, trying, experimenting, and involving as many other people as possible.

Stagnant organizations are typically led by individuals who place themselves in charge of ideas. These managers opt to share that responsibility with only a small number of people, if they are willing to share at all. Rarely will these men and women listen to their most trusted employees and they listen even less to their customers. That the employees in the pits and on the line offer a rich source of ideas on how to improve the quality of the product or service is inconceivable to these managers.

When they fail and end up in bankruptcy court it was, they say, the bad breaks and unfair competition that did them in. Most go to their deaths unaware that they plowed barren ground only feet above a mother lode of natural resources that could have engendered unimaginable achievement.

**Timing**

In leadership, as in hitting a baseball, timing is everything. The best swing in the world will produce no hits if the ball is already in the catcher's mitt. Opportunities, in this respect, are much like baseballs. When they come your way you had better be ready to capitalize because when they are gone, they are gone.

Unlike baseballs, the arrival of opportunities is much less predictable. The key, therefore, to taking advantage of opportunities is to be able to recognize them when they come and take advantage of them when recognized. Preparation is a pre-requisite of timing. The proper time to prepare one's self is now. Not tomorrow, nor next week, nor next month, but now!

Yes, I understand that now may not be perfect timing. John in engineering may be off for a couple of days and Mary in R & D may be committed to another project, but start preparing anyway because opportunities do not care an iota whether the time is convenient, let alone perfect. They come unannounced and those who are prepared prosper. Those of us caught napping, lose out.

Now may not be the perfect time for action but it is always the best time. Does that mean rush blindly forward? No! Taking action means implementing a strategy and sometimes the strategy may involve taking preliminary steps but keep in mind that delaying implementation is always a calculated risk. You certainly cannot wait until conditions are perfect. Generally, people wait because they are afraid to act and almost anything becomes an acceptable excuse to delay. Delay action only when waiting creates a strategic or tactical advantage.

Action-oriented people, on the other hand, have no fear of action. They may weigh the strategic pros and cons and decide to do A and B before C and D and they do this with the full knowledge that there is risk involved. Most of the time, action-oriented, positive leaders realize the best approach is often the quick and dirty one.

**Greatness**

Talent, confidence, commitment, integrity, hard work, determination, practice, enthusiasm, competitiveness, fun, poise, persistence, and toughness are just a few of the characteristics of champion athletes. Whatever the endeavor the attributes of greatness are constant.

Talent is not bequeathed equally and some champions have more than others. They each possess enough to succeed, however.

Confidence is crucial because it acknowledges the talent and engenders belief that all is possible, that objectives are achievable.

Commitment implies that doing the thing is at the top of one's priority list. Goals and objectives that rank low on the priority list are there for a reason. They should not be ignored but neither should they draw focus away from items at the top of our list.

The need for integrity may seem an unlikely one. Its importance cannot be underestimated, however. Faithful adherence to one's values provides emotional security and equilibrium. More than one championship has been lost from the invisible impact of emotional distractions.

All great performers possess self-discipline. They are devoted to the development of healthy minds and bodies. They resist the temptations that would interfere with their regimen and with their commitment.

Enthusiasm for effort and the game are ever-present among positive leaders. They thrive on the quest, the challenge, and the competition. It fulfills them and sustains them and gives them the energy so essential for success.

Energy is converted to action through work. Without hard work, hard jobs go undone and difficult objectives go unmet. Champions demonstrate their commitment and dedication by their hard work.

Determination is an extension of commitment but is so important that it is treated separately. Determined people refuse to let obstacles get in their way and they refuse to accept defeat or become discouraged by setbacks.

Practice may not really make perfect but it is the only thing that allows one to approach perfection. Practice is the essence of preparation and unless one is prepared to take advantage of an opportunity, it will pass one by. Practice hones the skills and refines the talents, enabling us to approach our potential. Practice is where we learn from our mistakes and where mistakes have only positive consequences. (An unfortunate fact in the education of our children is that we grade their practices (homework) and count their mistakes against them).

Competitiveness is nothing more than the love of action. It is the burning inward desire to play the game, to achieve, to excel, to perform, and to win. Competitiveness is the virtuous side of aggression.

Seeing the challenge as a game puts things in their proper perspective and helps the performer have poise under pressure. Poise is steadiness under fire—calm under pressure. Champions look forward to the moment of truth. They dream about it and visualize a successful outcome. Their poise allows them to focus their talent and preparation on the task or objective, unfettered by the distractions of the moment.

Champions are persistent. Champions do not give up and are discouraged by neither fear nor failure. They are resilient and able to regroup and try again, applying the lessons of experience.

Finally, champions are tough. They do whatever must be done and do not back off just because the job is unpleasant, difficult, or painful. Neither do they back off because people with whom they must interact are difficult.

Be tough but do not humiliate. Be tough but do not belittle. Be tough but do not abuse. Remember always the purpose of the endeavor: to strengthen, improve, to teach, or facilitate. Your job is to help people be successful and this requires a physical, intellectual, emotional, and spiritual toughness.

These are just a few of the attributes of great leaders in any of life's venues. You can achieve greatness, too. Do it by utilizing your full potential and by giving fully of yourself without reservation or regret. Remember, as we look back on our lives, it is not the things we tried and failed that are regretted but the things we failed to try. A cliché, I know, but oh so true.

If you are dissatisfied with your own life, examine your attributes. How do they measure up? It is these attributes that determine your achievements—your greatness.

**Honesty**

Do honesty and integrity have meaning today? Are we becoming an amoral society? More and more it appears that expediency is the most precious value of our era.

We despair of the social problems facing our society: drug and alcohol abuse, violence, hunger, poverty, materialism, homelessness, rampant racial and religious bigotry and hatred, widespread hetero- and homosexual promiscuity (only somewhat diminished by the AIDS pandemic), and economic and ecological problems that stagger the imagination. We claim great concern about these issues and lament their worsening, always asking why.

At one time or another, each of these problems is cited as the cause of our moral decay but they are clearly not the cause. Each of these crises, and many more not listed, are nothing more than symptoms of a more fundamental ailment. Our system of morals and values have been neglected to an ever-expanding degree for at least a half century, creating as many as two full generations of young people with an insufficient moral anchor to guide and protect them.

Think in terms of rearing a child. It is well established that children flourish in an environment where there are clear guidelines, consistent discipline, and loving care. Generations require the same nurturing if they are to preserve and protect the dominant values and concepts of right and wrong. Recent generations have heard lip service to our society's values systems but they have seen something altogether different. They have witnessed hypocrisy and also a willingness to sacrifice those values whenever it is expedient or, when it serves one's self-interest, a willingness to ignore or disregard them for selfish purposes.

Re-examine the evidence. There are many Americans who cheat on their tax returns; make false claims to their insurance companies; steal from employers; walk out of hotels with a suitcase full of contraband; shoplift; exceed the speed limit by substantial amounts and violate other traffic laws. We have all heard of business owners who turn off the cash register, frequently, so as to under-report their receipts; of corporate officers who sacrifice the best interests of their shareholders and employees for their own personal best interests.

We talk about values to our children but we set an entirely different example and our actions speak far more eloquently than our words. We have taught our children well, although the lessons they have learned were other than that which we intended. The moral and ethical values that made our nation special and upon which our grandparents were reared in the secure discipline of consistency have been notably absent. As a result, our children drift away from a moral pathway and they feel helpless, powerless, alone, and confused.

We have created teeming cities with degenerating school systems that breed millions of young people for whom there is little hope and even less chance of entering and succeeding in the mainstream of society, whether economically, intellectually, or socially. These cancerous, blighted areas grow at a rate far faster than the ability of the mainstream to carry the burden and are populated by men and women who have not only lost hope themselves but do not teach their children to hope. They do not teach their children that a better life is attainable nor do they help them develop the motivation and other tools essential to even envision, let alone grasp the dream. Educated Americans flee by the millions to suburbs, depriving the cities of the benefit of their tax resources.

It has got to stop! If we fail to act quickly to turn this situation around, it will consume us as surely as a cancerous growth in our belly, left unattended, will consume our bodies. Things must change and change dramatically!

The problem has evolved to the point that there are no easy answers and no inexpensive solutions. The price will be steep and we must all share in its payment. There can be no exceptions and no exemptions. What we require is a transformation and a renewed commitment to an old value system. Not turning back the clock! Not living in the past! The solution is simply repackaging our traditional values in late twentieth-century wrapping. We must restore in each American a commitment to our community.

Teenagers and young adults today, in far too many places, seem woefully lacking in basic skills and, more importantly, in the strong self-discipline and work ethic that built our democratic society. Yet many of these virtues are notably present in the workforces of the emerging economic powers who compete with America in the world's markets—who compete with America for economic prosperity.

Somehow, as a people, we must rediscover these virtues. The potential consequence of our inaction is the loss of the pre-imminence the U.S. has enjoyed for over a century. My prediction is that, as a result of our inaction, by the middle of the twenty-first century, China will turn to the United States as its source of cheap labor.

**Commitment Is the Key**

Successful leadership in today's economic environment requires a major commitment. In addition to the great things a committed leader can accomplish for his or her company, for its people, and the economy, marvelous things will accrue for him or her, individually. The intrinsic rewards are also substantial. It is exhilarating and fulfilling to be involved in something important that is bigger than us. Positive leaders may work long and hard but it is an uplifting rather than an exhausting experience. It leaves him or her with a positive attitude, a happy outlook, and with plenty of energy to devote to family and other social relationships and obligations.

It is also necessary that we spend time talking about quitters. Quitting is a sickness in the sense that it seems to have a power or control over people. It drains the energy from one's spirit. Quitting is always the easiest way out of a tough situation and it is always easy to rationalize. Anyone can quit and many do. The saying, "When the going gets tough, the tough get going!" has much wisdom to it. In a previous section we discussed the difficulty in starting something, the awesome power of inertia. It is equally challenging to stick to a project when difficulties arise. Most efforts devoted to worthwhile objectives will inevitably meet with innumerable obstacles, any one of which can kill the initiative if we are not diligent.

Quitting is also one of the worst things in the world for our peace of mind. There are few things that haunt us like looking back on life and regretting the opportunities that slipped by because we gave up prematurely, because we quit. It is agonizing because there is nothing we can do about it when it is over. Nothing, that is, except learn from the experience, and resist the temptation to give up on subsequent opportunities and challenges, too soon.

But when is too soon? There are times when the best thing to do is to walk away from a lost cause, to cut our losses and get out of a losing situation. How does one differentiate between quitting and an appropriate cessation or concession? There is no easy answer. What we can say is that quitting is an emotional decision made when we feel defeated. Terminating a lost cause is a rational decision made in the context of dynamic priorities and exigencies.

One must do what one must do. We lose more opportunities, mischannel more energy and create more ill-will by procrastinating, or worse, by never getting around to action. So act! Get after it. Letting things pile up inevitably results in the feeling of being overwhelmed—hence powerless—by it all. Staying on top of things contributes to the feeling of being in control. It stands to reason that we think and act more creatively and productively when we feel in control of a situation as opposed to feeling overwhelmed by it.

Commitment is a powerful tool that enables people to overcome obstacles and achieve objectives. It is many things: determination, courage, tenacity, self-discipline, drive, passion, relentlessness. Commitment is the thing that finally helps the smoker kick the habit after scores of half-hearted attempts. It happens at the gut level. It occurs when a want or a desire is converted to a need. Commitment is the stuff of which success is made.

Commitment forces us to pay the price of success. It is an esteem builder or destroyer according to how it is employed. If we make commitments and accept responsibility for them, our esteem is enhanced through a sense of accomplishment; through the feeling of having power over our own destiny. Avoidance of commitment is nothing more than shunning responsibility. Our esteem is diminished as a result and we feel guilt and regret that eats at us throughout our lifetime. It saps our confidence and, over time, leaves us feeling helpless and powerless in the face of life's obstacles and challenges.

Positive leaders are committed to the success of their venture and to the values that drive it and they demand that same commitment from all members of their team. The level of their achievement is directly proportional to the level of their commitment and their relentless desire to share that commitment with others. How would you describe your commitment?

## *seven*

## UNDERSTANDS THAT SUCCESS IS A PROCESS

"I shall study and prepare myself and some day my chance will come."
— *Abraham Lincoln*

"As they, while others slept, struggled upward in the night."
— *Henry David Thoreau*

"Act boldly and unseen forces will come to your aid."
— *Dorothea Brande*

People dream about success and fantasize about doing great things. Many young people grow up dreaming about instant success, which they often confuse with wealth and fame, but never achieve it in real life because they do not know how. Some children live in a state of perpetual affluence and are required to contribute little, if anything at all, toward the maintenance of that affluence. They grow up taking affluence for granted. Others see affluence from afar and grow up dreaming of that affluence, perceiving it as success, but having no conception of the process through which it is achieved. They want to win the lottery or become an instant millionaire through professional athletics. Few of these children know how to convert their dreams to plans to action.

Even many adults think that success is a state of perpetual affluence and do not realize that success has nothing to do with affluence. It may well be true that affluence often follows success and that, in fact, successful people are frequently affluent but, in truth, material well being is simply a probable by-product of successful living. Often, our dreams for the future—our vision of what our life can be—are formed, not by rich values taught through the daily love, care, and discipline of our families but by the illusionary world of television and cinema, and through interaction with our peers. We oversimplify, of course, but the institutions of family, church, and school, which have been the traditional distilleries of American values, are not competing successfully for the attention, respect, and loyalty of our children. Far too many of our young people are not learning the things that they most need to know!

Millions of our young people embark upon their lives poorly equipped to meet its challenges. They are like buildings of an earlier era, thrown up hastily and without the solid foundation of values and the strong infrastructure of self discipline, work ethic, wisdom, and knowledge to withstand the stress of life's tremors, which will come as surely as the sunset.

Many American men and women are unhappy with their lives, with both their relationships and their careers. We want more from our relationships and more from our jobs. We want more friends, more money, more loving spouses, more power, more authority, more control, and more freedom! We want more success! This powerful drive for more success contributes to countless divorces and multiple job and career changes, and, in most cases, unnecessarily so. For most of us such changes are unnecessary. Contrary to common belief it is we—yes, you and me—and not some external force that keeps us from attaining the success to which we aspire.

The vast majority of you who are reading this page have the ability within you to succeed right where you are, just by doing things differently; by learning the process of success and by rededicating yourselves to positive values. You can improve your performance on the job, enhance your career, have a more satisfying marriage, and get more joy and meaning out of life. These things can happen, now!

Success is a process, not a state of being. It is neither wealth nor fame. Success is a fleeting thing not unlike a flame that burns as long as it has a steady supply of fuel. When we stop feeding fuel to the fire the flame dies out. People of all ages and backgrounds need to understand that success is attainable. Success is a methodology that can be learned by anyone with normal intelligence just as surely as anyone with normal eyesight, balance, and motor skills can learn to ride a bicycle. People need, desperately, to learn that the process of success is a skill that can give them a fairly high level of control over their own destiny; that it is a process that will give them incredible power to bring about positive change in their lives and in the world around them.

Webster's defines success as "a favorable or satisfactory outcome or result." For our purpose, success is "achieving objectives through positive action." Positive leaders consistently achieve their objectives and help other people do the same; hence, they experience success routinely.

It does not matter, in the abstract, to what goals one aspires. If you achieve those goals through positive action then you have achieved success. Success can be personal, interpersonal, or organizational but it is always tied to clearly delineated objectives and is always measured within the context of our relationships with other people.

**The Process**

What, then, is this process of success? It includes a mission in life, rooted in positive, life-affirming values; a positive attitude and approach to life; passion; a vision of how things can be; specific goals and objectives; an implementation plan; and finally, action. Success is that simple but it does not stop there. It is an infinite or incessant process. Action creates change. Change requires that the vision be re-examined, that the progress be measured, that the goals and objectives be adjusted, that the action plan be re-engineered, and that our actions themselves be modified accordingly. The process is repeated until we have converted the dream to reality, until we are satisfied. But satisfaction does not come easily, if it comes at all, and it is always temporary.

The more we accomplish, the more we learn, and the more we learn the more we imagine. What is vital is that our values, those core principles that sustain us, are not altered but remain rock solid.

**Mission**

Success in life begins with an unwavering commitment to a mission in life, a broad goal that spans a lifetime, and with an unfaltering adherence to a set of core values. These serve as the fulcrum that maintains equilibrium between actions and values and that guides the individual or enterprise. Your mission is much broader than goals and objectives and it is this mission that gives one a sense of direction and facilitates selection of specific goals and objectives. Your mission is the big picture; it is what you believe in—what you stand for. It is the reason you play the game.

What happens to most of us is that we do not think with sufficient frequency about our core values. They recede to the back of our consciousness where they are taken for granted and where they are allowed to play a minimal role in defining our actions. Often, we lose sight of them altogether or they become so distorted that they cannot have a positive influence on our actions.

Recall our earlier discussion on integrity. We all know right from wrong but few of us really take the time to critique our behavior against the benchmark of our core beliefs. Instead we rationalize. "Sure, I believe it is wrong to cheat and I consider myself to be an honest person. But, yes, I fudge a little on my taxes, after all, everyone does it and it does not really hurt anyone. And sure, every now and then I sneak a few extra office supplies from work but the company can afford it and they are not paying me what I'm worth anyway. And, of course, I pad my insurance claims once in a while but doesn't everyone? Besides, those insurance companies are rich with what they charge in premiums."

The examples are endless. After a while, we have compromised our values to the point that they no longer influence our behavior in a positive way and to the extent they once did.

Businesses that become obsessed with making money are a case in point. They sacrifice their mission for short-term profits and, in the process, erode the strength of the enterprise, often threatening its very existence. One of the common causes of business failure is this very phenomenon. The business sacrifices its commitment to quality and customer satisfaction for short-term gains and scores the point but loses the game.

Customer satisfaction must be the mission of every business enterprise and it can only be achieved through rigid adherence to core values and a commitment to quality products and services. Businesses that are loyal to this mission may experience short-term losses occasionally but will win in the long run. Companies that sacrifice their values may experience short-term prosperity but will ultimately fail. It is these core values that drive you and sustain you.

A leader with a clear sense of vision may be forced to deviate from his plan in the face of practical realities but each modification and adjustment is done in such a way to bring his life or the organization back on course. When the market changes so dramatically that a change in the mission is required, an event that is inevitable in the real world, the positive leader re-evaluates the marketplace and redefines the mission before proceeding.

The mission and its corresponding values not only guide the enterprise they drive it. Only when these are clearly defined and clearly and consistently communicated can specific goals and objectives be developed. Of the three: mission, vision, and values, mission is the most volatile as we must continually adapt to changes in the world and marketplace. Our vision of the world and our future is less dynamic but even visions must remain connected to a reality that never ceases to change. Our values, however, must be deeply rooted in order to withstand the incessant winds of change and keep us grounded. People who are not grounded by deeply rooted core values often see their personal and business lives ravaged.

**Positive Attitude**

One cannot conceive of success, let alone attain it, without a positive attitude that surveys the world and sees a universe full of possibilities.

The "positive principle" is an inherent part of the process of success because the successful achievement of goals and objectives cannot be accomplished unless we believe in their possibility.

Everything we do, every action we take and all that we think is filtered and colored by the vision we have of the world and of our life. Whether that vision is one of darkness and despair or light and hope is for us to choose. This picture represents the possibilities of our life as they exist in our mind, in our imagination. This image lives at multiple levels of our consciousness. Most importantly, we control it. We choose our vision whether we know it or not.

Our positive frame of mind gives us the courage of our convictions and the confidence in our talents. It enables us to risk defeat and to reach for the stars. Imagine if you will the surgeon who, in spite of all the training, is unable to cut into living, breathing human tissue. What good is the talent? What good is any talent without a belief in the possibilities and the courage of our convictions?

**Passion**

Highly successful people, almost always, are driven to succeed, often to the neglect of other aspects of their lives. The thing at which they excel is a passion and it consumes all their time and energy through most, if not all, of their lives. Positive leaders are passionate people. They are passionately dedicated to their values and are committed, fervently, to their life's mission. The challenge for passionate people is to keep their life in balance.

We need men and women who are passionate about positive values but those values must include passion for the people in their lives. Passion means feeling so strongly about something that you are willing to make sacrifices for it, to experience pain and suffering for the cause. It means caring about something so much that you are willing to give totally of yourself.

Very few individuals, however, are called to such a high cause that they are asked to sacrifice their personal lives and relationships. Most of us can have the best of both worlds and our mission in life should include being a caring partner, a nurturing parent, a good role model, a good friend, as well as a good provider.

Our career is a tool that enables us to care and provide for our families. We need to be passionate about doing our jobs well and be dedicated to our career but we are in disequilibrium if we permit that drive to cloud our purpose. Live passionately but be passionate about the things closest to your heart.

**Vision/Goals**

Our vision of the world has multiple dimensions. On the one hand, it is a grand vision that projects the full panorama; on the other, it is a seemingly infinite variety of specific thoughts, ideas, and feelings. Everything that has ever occurred in the history of the human species and that was initiated by human beings, whether significant or not, was spawned from the imagination (vision) of an individual man or woman. From the first use of a tool, the mastery of fire, the first artistic rendering, the first criminal act; all were conceived in the human mind.

We know that a vision is dynamic. Its basic outlines are drafted in our formative years and are fleshed out during the maturation process but the picture is never complete. For as long as we live, the vision is altered and reshaped by our life experiences and by our own will.

If the vision is positive we see our life and future in positive terms. We envision activities and achievements in the context of the big picture and this shapes the things we do and the decisions we make. We begin to lay the foundation for the realization of our vision for our lives. Unlike other living species, as far as we know at this time in history, we possess the ability to conceptualize and to think analytically.

The broad picture contains many scenes that lead us through the dimensions of our life and each scene is a vision of a possibility that we can turn into a reality. As we strive to transform each small vision, some work out and some do not, so we continuously revise and revamp, we adjust and modify the immediate scenes. Each adjustment slightly alters the big picture as well. At each step of the way we learn about ourselves and about the physical universe in which we live and this too shapes our vision at all levels.

As we achieve our goals, or abandon them, they are replaced by new goals. At any given point in our lives, the process of success requires that we have at least one and probably several active goals. If we have no goals we stagnate. Positive leaders are never complacent. They relentlessly strive to embody their vision and have multiple goals established for both their personal and organizational lives.

**Objectives/Actions**

Goal achievement is accomplished through objectives, which are the action steps in the process. Objectives must be specific and measurable and must have deadlines or completion dates. They must clearly serve the mission and must be consistent with the underlying value system.

The process is an indispensable tool of leadership. Leadership, in fact, cannot exist without this process. Positive leaders package this process of success in what we refer to as the "action strategy;" specifically action plans and action proposals. As we have already discussed, everyone has dreams but leaders have visions. Visions are dreams with wings, as Jack Frick, a trainer in the insurance industry liked to say. Visions are possibilities and require an accompanying action strategy.

Objectives are implemented through specific action plans and action proposals. The action plan is the goal-oriented, objective-based activity we devise for our own implementation. It outlines the specific steps we plan to take to achieve the results we desire. Action plans may include action proposals. Action proposals are the tool we use to sell our mission/vision to other people and to enlist them in the effort.

If we intend to accomplish a certain goal, it requires that we implement certain actions. These actions are not random; they are organized in a specific way that we believe will enable us to achieve our goal. Positive leaders work to develop the skill of preparing action plans in some detail. Most are written, some exist only in our mind.

If we want to accomplish a certain objective that involves the cooperation of other people we cannot assume that they will automatically come to our assistance. We must ask for their help and we must share our vision and goals to garner their support. We do this through the action proposal. Action proposals are effective at all levels of an organization whether we are the CEO or the most junior member of the team. When we see a problem we seek a solution and solutions require implementation. Once we have thought the process through in our mind, we prepare a simple action proposal that defines the problem and outlines specific goals, objectives, and action steps. The action proposal, which can be as brief as one piece of paper, is submitted to someone who has the power to authorize its implementation.

Whether each and every action proposal is accepted is unimportant. What is of vital importance is that they are prepared and submitted because they make good things happen. That they draw positive attention to the proponent is also noteworthy.

Here is a list of good things that can result from a well-conceived action proposal:

- The proposal can gain the approval of management and be implemented.
- It may serve as a catalyst that sparks a better idea in someone else's imagination.
- Like the idea that's time is not ripe, it may be filed away in the memory of the organization, only to re-emerge at a later date at which time it has a dramatic positive impact.
- It will identify the initiator as a problem-solver; as a leader; as a pro-active, positive force in the organization; as a doer.
- It will set an example to others as a positive way to make things happen.

The one characteristic of positive leaders that stands out is this propensity for action. It is this willingness to act that is the essence of leadership.

"To lead" and "to go first" are action verbs. True leaders are people who take action regardless of their position within the organization. Many formal leaders (managers and supervisors), however, do their best to avoid taking action. They put off decisions, delay action on recommendations, and overlook people problems; hoping the problems will go away.

Effective leaders, on the other hand, believe the best solution to a problem is to act quickly and at the lowest possible level. When they see a problem, they accept responsibility for it. Then, they take action. If the initial action strategies do not work or produce less than optimal results, we try something else until we get a satisfactory outcome, however long it takes. When the perfect solution is not possible—and they rarely are—we settle for an imperfect solution. Rarely do positive leaders worry about mistakes or failures because they understand that, in the real world, mistakes and failures are the stepping stones to success. Every mistake and failed attempt provides an opportunity to learn and this new knowledge significantly enhances the probability that subsequent action will be successful.

Reflect on your own experience. At one time or another each of us has worked with managers who lead and managers who avoid leadership. Which worked best? Which was the most fun?

What kind of leader are you? Remember, leaders act; they take responsibility; they tinker; they do not worry about mistakes provided the mistake is an honest one resulting from a good try, or that teaches a valuable lesson.

You are faced with a promotion decision. What attributes do you seek? Look for the person who demonstrates leadership. He or she will be easy to recognize. These men and women never complain about things, they suggest solutions to make things better. They are always trying something new; always looking for a new and better way to improve the quality of the product or service or the productivity of their unit.

Successful organizations are populated throughout by people who accept responsibility for solving problems and for implementing and continually modifying strategies and action plans. These organizations are action-oriented. Action converts dreams to reality. More specifically, action converts ideas into marketable products and services.

Effective leaders exhibit a special ability to act quickly. These men and women analyze problems on the spot; solicit input from line staff, supply chain partners, and from any other direct participants they can find; then, they act to implement a solution or to empower others to do so.

The most effective leaders do not make all decisions, nor are they the only people entitled to take action. More often than not the leader's contribution to action is to encourage, sometimes demand that their people take action. They facilitate the process, eliminate barriers, cut through red tape, provide protection from outside criticism or interference, and provide emotional support. They also forgive mistakes, applaud nice tries, and encourage their people to pick up the pieces (clean up their mess) and try again. Effective leaders empower people and teach and guide them through the process of success.

Many managers view themselves as effective, action-oriented leaders because of their ability to swoop in during times of crisis like the Lone Ranger and take quick and decisive action. Even when the results of these activities are consistently good, these managers can do harm to their organizations. How? By sending a tainted message to their people suggesting that only the boss can solve problems. People in these organizations are immobilized in crisis situations and become totally dependent upon the leader. They are taught that problem solving is someone else's responsibility.

The leader's responsibility extends beyond just action and solutions to include developing these abilities in their people. The effective leader's positive expectations of his or her people and their ability to solve problems can produce astonishing results. These men and women inevitably preside over an action-oriented organization that continuously experiments with new and better ideas and rarely misses growth or market opportunities because of the inability to act. Neither do these leaders pass on the opportunity to re-invent their organizations. The entities over which they preside are truly learning organizations in which every member of the team shares in the responsibility for meeting customer expectations. In learning organizations, every member of the team understands how what they do fits into the grand scheme of things and is a potential source of knowledge, ideas, and inspiration.

How would you rate your organization? Is it bureaucratic or is the leadership primed to act. Does it encourage its people to take responsibility for making things happen? How do you measure up to these standards in the eyes of your people?

Action proposals are an alternative to complaints. Imagine, if you will, an organization brimming with people who do not complain about problems but offer solutions, instead. The difference is phenomenal. People who offer solutions think in terms of possibilities and probabilities and they accept responsibility for their environment. People who complain think in terms of obstacles and barriers and the impossibilities pollute their mind. They not only deny responsibility for their environment, they feel powerless.

In which world would you rather live and work?

People tend to reject the notion that they can have this kind of power; that anything they do could ever influence the people around them. Their rejection is based on their own feelings of inadequacy and their lack of understanding of the way people behave and respond in organizations and also their lack of a positive attitude. It is based on their inability to understand and master the process of success. Look around you! Everything you see that is man-made exists only because someone had a vision and breathed life into that vision.

Believe it and you acquire enormous power. Work hard to master the skill of developing and presenting (selling) action proposals designed to solve the problems you see in your environment—to make your part of the world a better place, not just for you but for everyone—and you will see that power accomplish astonishing things.

**Accept the Challenge**

People spend their whole lives dreaming about success, never learning how to achieve it because they have not learned how to convert their dreams to specific goals and objectives, to plans and, finally, to action.

Success is the process of achieving goals and objectives through positive action. When one set of objectives are accomplished they must be replaced with new goals lest the flame of success die out. It is an incessant process. We have all seen persons who have achieved much in their lives but arrive at a point in which they see nothing more to be accomplished. Gradually, they begin to stagnate; growing more and more depressed and discouraged with their lives. If allowed to continue unimpeded, this decaying process will sap that person of their vitality, their energy, and even their will to live.

We must revise our goals and objectives, constantly; replacing, updating, and always converting new dreams to new plans to new action. Only thus can we preserve our vitality and our enthusiasm for life, keeping the flame of success burning ever brightly.

Functionally speaking, success is neither good nor bad. One can successfully achieve a bad objective; one can be a good thief. One could say that John Dillinger was a successful man, as was Adolph Hitler. We may choose to pass judgment on the product of their effort but their achievements were the product of the process of success. They had specific objectives, they had action plans, and they implemented those plans with all of the energy and resources available to them.

They were successful in their own mind and this is the important point. One cannot measure success by the expectation of others but must seek to be successful in one's own mind. People who always seek acclaim from others are seldom happy. It is only when they seek to satisfy themselves that they can be happy and successful. Yet, at the same time, because we are living, breathing human beings our social relationships are of paramount importance to us. We derive our greatest joy and fulfillment through our relationships with other people. Even success at the most personal level would seem somehow hollow if we were unable to share it with others. Remarkably, it is so much easier to satisfy the other people in our lives once we are satisfied with ourselves.

## Handling the Ups and Downs

How you respond to the bad days, losses, failures, mistakes, and bad fortune speaks volumes about your character, your leadership style, and competency. Everyone has days when things go wrong but winners recognize that such setbacks, taken in the context of the whole, are relatively meaningless and they forget quickly about such times. Positive Leaders have short memories in that they dwell on neither their success nor their failures.

If it was a loss or failure to perform, winners do not get down on themselves but, instead, clinically evaluate their performance and take corrective action. They recognize that the key to success is not wanting things to be different but doing something to make things different.

Ask yourself: "What can I do about the situation?" Then, as the Nike ads once suggested, "Just Do It!"

Recognize that, more often than not, failure or poor performance is a function of preparation. The better prepared one is the more likely one is to perform well.

The flip side of controlling your response to tough times is maintaining an even keel when you are on a roll. When things are going well it is easy to take quality performance for granted and begin to think it unnecessary to continue working hard to perform well. Over confidence, cockiness, and complacency have been the undoing of many talented people who let winning go to their head.

Again, athletics provides an analogy. It is more difficult to defend a championship than it is to attain the initial victory. When the athlete is hungry for victory it is easy for them to maintain their focus on the process of preparing for competition. Once the championship has been won, it is not uncommon for the champion to lose a little of the edge that brought him or her to the winner's circle. It takes a championship effort to rededicate oneself to the same regimen that produced victory and not everyone is willing to do that.

What separates winners and losers, then, is that winners understand that success is a process. Winners enjoy their victories but preserve their focus on the discipline of winning. The process of success necessarily includes a few roller coaster rides through the highs and lows of life. Positive leaders do not permit the transitory highs and lows of life to affect their focus on their destination.

**Principles of Successful People**

Recently, Consultant Brian Tracy spoke at a conference for credit union executives and my brother passed them on to me. Tracy's *Ten Principles That Successful People Live By*[27]:

1. **The Principle of Purpose**
    -A purpose is your reason why you do what you do.
    -Without a clearly defined sense of purpose, there is no way to develop and maintain self-esteem.
2. **The Principle of Excellence**
    -When you make a decision to be the best is when you begin to become excellent.
    -Excellence is the core of self-esteem.
3. **The Principle of Responsibility**
    -Our life begins to move ahead when we accept 100% responsibility for ourselves – when we stop making excuses.
    -In life, the only thing you can control is what you do and say and think and feel. Everything else is controlled by external forces.
    -*Change is constant; difficulty is constant; problems are constant. The only thing we can decide is how we will respond to these.*
4. **The Principle of Service**
    -We only grow great in life to the degree to which we lose ourselves in serving other people.
    -The Law of Compensation states that you never get more out of your relationships, family, children, work and health than you put into them.
5. **The Principle of Self-Development**

---
[27] Brian Tracy is an internationally renown motivational speaker, www.briantracy.com

-You only work for yourself. You are in charge of your research and development and upgrading yourself. You are the architect of your own destiny.
-You are self-made.

6. **The Principle of Concentration**
    -Every successful man or woman has developed the ability to concentrate on one thing at a time.

7. **The Principle of Cooperation**
    -85% of your success in life is determined by your interpersonal skills.
    -The more you like yourself, the more you will like others. The more you like others, by the Principle of Reciprocation, the more they will like you; and the more they like you, the more they want to do things for you.

8. **The Principle of Creativity**
    -You can never advance in life any further than you have advanced today except by working smarter.
    -Every problem has a solution.

9. **The Principle of Integrity**
    -Live in truth.
    -Each person has a conscience, a block of laws that tells you what is right or wrong. When you listen to this inner voice, your self-esteem goes up.

10. **The Principle of Courage**
    -Fear of failure holds most people back from trying.
    -You cannot avoid problems and setbacks. They are a natural part of life.
    -Go confidently in the direction of your dreams; act as if it were impossible to fail.

**Other Characteristics**

PREPARATION
COMMITMENT
HARD WORK

DEDICATION
DISCIPLINE
PERSISTENCE

These words are just a few that characterize highly successful people. These individuals are at the peak of their art or craft. How do they do it? Well, of course, they have talent—but then lots of people have talent. The world is full of talented people who think back on opportunities in their lives and say, "with a little luck I might have made it!"

But all talented people do not make it, and luck may or may not deserve credit for the outcome. We all have good luck but we are not all prepared to capitalize on it when it comes. Conversely, everyone experiences bad luck in their lives but how many of us deal with adversity, well?

They say winners make their own breaks and this we have found to be especially true. Those of us who blame everything on bad luck are not accepting responsibility for the outcomes in our lives. If we reflect on the opportunities that have come our way we discover that they often come unexpectedly, catching us off guard and unprepared.

We might say it was bad luck that good fortune, in the guise of opportunity, called upon us when we were not ready but it's not really bad luck at all—it is little more than lack of readiness. Establish goals and objectives for yourselves.

Make a **commitment** to those goals and **dedicate** yourself to doing everything in your power to facilitate them. **Work hard** to develop your skills and **discipline** yourself to a regimen that will maximize your talents and energies toward that end.

Be **persistent** in spite of the obstacles that present themselves and the setbacks that befall you. Follow the Boy Scout motto and "*Be Prepared.*" Know that all the work and all the effort you put forth is **preparation** for the time when opportunity knocks so that it will not catch you napping. And, when opportunities appear, take **positive action** using all the skills and abilities in your arsenal and all the energy at your command.

Does all this guarantee success in all that you attempt? No! There are no guarantees in life. It does, however, improve the odds so dramatically in your favor that successes become probabilities rather than possibilities. Teach yourself the process and make success a probability in your life!

Take action now! Master the process of success and you will begin to experience success and achieve results almost immediately. Do not wait and hope that success will happen in your life, some day. Make it happen and "put wings on your dreams."

## *eight*

## UNDERSTANDS MOTIVATION

Motivating people is the primary responsibility of leadership. For the positive leader, motivating people is a relatively simple challenge. It is very much like magic. All one must do to make it happen is to believe.

The key to human motivation in the workforce, or anywhere else for that matter, is simply "make people feel important!"

That's all there is to it. Make people feel important. Unbelievably simple, isn't it? Well, believe it! Every human being alive wants to feel important. Leaders who successfully convey that they consider their people important are highly likely to succeed.

Examine your own experience with your favorite supervisor or teacher. You felt a special relationship with your mentor, a real kinship. You knew you were liked and you did your best work while they were involved in your life. What did they do differently than the other teachers and supervisors who clutter your memory?

They treated you as if you were special. They liked you. They remembered your name; they listened to you; they valued your opinion; they showed appreciation for your efforts; they smiled at you; they treated you with respect; they trusted you; they challenged you; they tried to help you do a better job; they let you make mistakes without fear of retribution or humiliation; they encouraged you to try again; they made sure you received full recognition for your contributions; they expected much from you; and so much more.

They made you feel important! It was no act. They believed it. It was a genuine feeling and it was easy because they liked you. Positive leaders genuinely care about their people and believe in their capabilities.

Believe this and act on it and you will produce magical results!

There will always be a few unproductive people no matter how capable their supervisor but they are the exception, not the norm. The overwhelming majority of employees can and will be both motivated and productive if you are an effective, positive leader. When they are not motivated and productive it is your responsibility, not that of society. You recruited them, you hired them and trained them and you evaluate them. It may well be that they came to your shop poorly prepared to live up to your expectations but they were the best of the lot. Once you signed them on, you accepted responsibility for their development and their performance and you retain that responsibility for as long as they remain a member of your team.

As a leader, the only meaningful measure of your success is how well you take this raw material and mold it into a well-trained, sharply focused, well-motivated workforce.

Supervisory leadership is one of the most under-rated, most unappreciated, and misunderstood skills in existence today. If our corporate leaders devoted half as much time and energy to the development of their leadership skills as they devote to their technical skills they would be astonished by all they could accomplish. Learn how to be a positive leader-manager by learning how to motivate people. It is easy once you acquire the genuine belief that your people are your most important asset and you communicate that fact to them through your words, your actions, and through the rules and structure of your organization. Make people feel important!

**Priorities**

Human motivation is a complex subject. For all the attention motivation has received over the years its critical role is under-appreciated.

What all the theories of motivation will tell you is that people are complex living organisms but, in fact, we all want pretty much the same things in life. Referring back to the quote from Norman Vincent Peale:

"What every one of us wants, more than anything else, is life. Life is vitality; it is energy; it is freedom; it is growth." (Peale, 1954).

If you want to be a successful leader then you must convey to your people that they are the most important resource available to you. When they begin to trust that they are valued by the organization and their boss; when they learn to trust that your role is to drive the organization toward its objectives by helping them succeed; when they come to realize that their ability to get what they want out of life is tied irrevocably to the success of the organization; when they truly believe these things you will have a motivated, positive workforce.

Organizations depend on people understanding one another. Understanding is based on trust. In the comic strip Shoe, the character named Skyler is a young fish hawk. While passing through the line in his school's cafeteria, Skyler observes that all of the food servers are wearing latex gloves, plastic hairnets, and masks. Skyler turns to his friend and says, "If they're afraid to touch it, I'm not going to eat it!" (MacNelly, Jeff, creator).

Poor Skyler, who went hungry that day, did not realize that the gloves and other protective gear were there for his benefit rather than for the protection of the people whose job it was to serve him. He did not realize it because leadership had not conveyed its mission and had not earned his trust.

For many people in leadership, rather than thinking of people as their most important and trusted asset, they are taught that labor is one of the biggest costs of doing business. They were not taught that people can rise to expectations and accept responsibility but rather that people cannot be trusted and that we need to take great precautions lest they loaf, sabotage the operation, or steal the organization blind. In one organization with which I had a consulting relationship, the plant manager told me, bluntly, that none of his employees could be trusted and he treated them like malingerers and thieves. So firm was he in his belief that he kept all of the supply cabinets locked and not even his shop supervisors and lead people were given keys. On one occasion, the plant manager was in a meeting with a prospective new customer and he had given emphatic instructions that he was not to be disturbed. As luck would have it, several of the assembly lines ran out of masking tape, which was critical to a specific step in the assembly process. As a result, those lines had to be shut down because no one had the key to the storage cabinets to access a couple of rolls of masking tape, worth about a buck each; and, no one would dare knock on the conference room door to ask for the keys.

The conventional wisdom of an earlier time was that one does not share critical information with one's people because it might confuse or upset them or, more likely, because they might not honor the need for confidentiality. It was believed that people do not really want to work hard and management must be prepared to crack the whip if they want to get anything close to a full day's production out of their people.

In a presentation to a national convention to which we earlier referred, consultant Brian Wilson talked about how to kill enthusiasm and creativity in your organization:

1. "Regard any ideas from the line with suspicion, just because it came from the line.
2. Insist on approvals from each layer. Don't let this person down here run in and tell you about this gem. Make sure you stop them in their tracks and make them go thru channels.
3. Ask departments and individuals to criticize each other and then just sit back and pick the survivors.
4. Express your criticism freely and withhold your praise.
5. Make sure requests for information are fully justified.
6. Assign to lower level managers, in the name of delegation and participation, responsibility for how to cut back, lay people off, move people around and make threatening decisions that we have made, but get them to do it quickly.
7. Don't forget that we already have all the answers."

So much of the conventional wisdom that guides our behavior is contrary to the idea that people are our most important resource.

Producing quality goods and services requires that the organization manage its resources efficiently and effectively. Those resources are:

- People
- Time
- Money

Time is important but by itself it just passes. Time contributes to the production of goods and services only when used efficiently by people. Money is also important but only relative to its utility to people. It takes people to make time and money productive.

I spent some time with the owner of a small but profitable company with only seven employees. The owner was constantly complaining about how difficult it was to get good help.

"No one wants to work anymore!" he cried. "They don't appreciate what a good thing they have, working here."

He wore his frustration out where everyone could see, which caused a great deal of consternation among his people.

"I can do every job in the company," he boasted, "better than my people!"

"I see," was my reply and then I asked, "How much are you paying these people?"

"Probably close to $200,000 per year," he responded, in shock as if he had seen that number for the first time. "My God!" he continued, "You would think for that kind of money I could buy some decent help."

I thought for a moment and then responded, "I think I've got a simple solution for you. In fact, it's so simple I'm surprised you haven't thought of it yourself."

He didn't say anything right away but just looked at me. Finally he asked, "How much is this going to cost me?"

"Well, it's such a simple solution I am almost embarrassed to charge you anything at all. But, since I would soon go broke if I gave away free advice, why don't I bill you for one hour of my time and we will call it even."

My client was skeptical but we shook hands on the deal. "Okay! What is this simple solution?"

"Just get rid of all of your staff," I announced, "and do all the work yourself! You do it better anyway and then you can pocket the $200,000 in payroll costs every year. Heck, in a few years you'll be able to retire on the money you save."

Needless to say, my client was not particularly happy with my suggestion and he, "damn sure wasn't going to pay me for a ridiculous piece of advice like that."

When he finally calmed down, we discussed his attitudes at some length because it was his attitude that was the problem. He finally acknowledged that he could not be everywhere at once or do all of the jobs at the same time and, in fact, after much gnashing of teeth, he admitted that he needed his people. He acknowledged that, in spite of all his knowledge and expertise he was incapable of running his business by himself.

As we talked about his attitudes, he began to see that the message he conveyed, daily, to his people was that they should be grateful for their jobs and to him for giving them jobs. He routinely conveyed his lack of appreciation for them and his lack of trust and respect for them. Not once had it occurred to him to thank his people or tell them how important their contributions were to the success of his business.

This simple discussion opened his eyes to a room full of other problems spawned by his attitude; problems that were sapping his organization of its strength, its vitality, and its potential for productivity, and creativity. Together, we worked to identify the negative messages so that he could begin to replace them with positive and affirming interactions with his people. What we identified were:

- He always boasted that he could do the job better than any of them were able,
- He talked only about what his people were unable to do rather than about their capabilities—he focused on their weaknesses rather than strengths,

- He frequently jumped into the fray at crucial times to insure that his people did not "screw up,"
- He rarely took time to teach people what he knew so they could become more proficient than he was.

The examples go on and on. Not surprisingly, a simple but dramatic change in his attitude toward his people and their importance sparked numerous positive changes in the culture of his organization. His people were skeptical of him at first, but once they recognized his sincerity and witnessed the consistency of his new message, his company took on a new life and a new personality. He learned that his job as leader was not to be the best at every single job rather it was to teach his people how to do those jobs as well as or even better than could he.

In one of the leadership seminars I have led, a participant asked the question: "How do I get my people to accept responsibility for getting things done when I am away from the job?" My answer was simple: "Teach them how to accept responsibility for getting things done while you are there." In other words, share responsibility with your people rather than horde it.

**Kissing the Baby**

Politicians are skilled at making people feel important, at least during their campaign for office. Making people feel important is how they get elected and, if they do it consistently well, get reelected. What politicians do is kiss their constituents' babies. Kissing babies is more than just a ritual and it represents, symbolically, the essence of motivating people. Nothing we do or say will swell an individual's pride more than kissing their babies, whether literally or figuratively.

Kissing babies means drawing positive, special attention to the thing(s) that are closest to a person's heart. If we do this with grace and sincerity we make people feel important and they will not forget us. Effective leaders develop the politician's skill at kissing babies. They pay attention to people and listen to them, empathically. Effective leaders pay attention to people in a positive and affirmative manner.

They listen to what people really say and they learn the things, actions, ideas, or opinions that the person holds most dear. At every opportunity, they single out people for positive attention.

In doing so, they create loyalties and trust; they make people feel needed and appreciated. When a positive leader requires a special effort, they can ask for it with full confidence that it will be forthcoming. When positive leaders need to help an individual learn something and grow from their mistakes, they find their people willing to listen and willing to make difficult changes. People are willing because they have learned to trust and respect their leader.

**Teach Them How to Win**

One of the most effective ways to make people feel important is to teach them how to be a winner. Everyone aspires to be a winner in life but few of us really know how to win or even understand what winning is all about. The leader who masters the ability to teach his or her people how to be successful in a competitive environment will have at his disposal one of the most powerful forces in the history of mankind—a highly motivated group of people.

Learning how to be a winner begins with the acknowledgement that the world is a highly competitive place in which to live. Competition has somehow acquired a bad name in much of contemporary thinking and this is unfortunate. The fact is that an ability to compete is essential in life. Competition is an inherent component of the natural world of living organisms and it is also a powerful motivational tool.

The problem with competition can be best illustrated by the "Little League" analogy, which we discussed in an earlier chapter. Indisputable abuses by parents of children participating in organized sports have led many to conclude that such activities are bad for children. Bad because the activities place children under the pressure of a competitive environment where winning appears to be the only thing that is important.

Critics and advocates alike acknowledge that it is the parents and coaches that are the problem. Instead of creating an environment where children can participate for enjoyment, with or without an adult audience, such competition places too much emphasis on the outcomes. The emphasis, critics suggest, should be on the enjoyment the activity brings and the role of adults, if anything at all, should be on teaching the fundamentals of the game. In part, these experts are correct but I believe they have given competition a bad name.

Unfortunately, as has been well-documented, parents and coaches see youth sports as an opportunity to live vicariously through their children; playing out their own personal fantasy of coaching a team to a championship. Most parents want their child to excel; to make the winning play. They want the child to be a star, "like old Dad once was," or more likely, like old Dad dreamt of being but never was.

Parents get upset when their child performs less stellarly than they wish or if they perceive that the child is treated unfairly. They are incensed with the coaches about the amount of playing time their child receives or about other coaching decisions. They become angry when the officiating is less professional than they think it should be.

It is bad enough that parents have these feelings. It is worse that they display them for the whole world to see, including their children. There is no question that these occurrences place unreasonable pressure on the young participant and spoil a great deal of the child's enjoyment. What is worse is that the child's sense of self worth begins to be colored by the level of their performance in activities that were never meant to be anything but a game and an opportunity to let a child experiment with a sporting activity.

With all these problems, it is no wonder that people are upset and speak out for discontinuation of such activities. These individuals jump to the conclusion that it is the competition that is an evil thing and that winning is unimportant. The problem is not competition nor is it undue emphasis on winning. Both winning and competition are good and vitally important things. The problem is immature adults who, as parents and coaches, do not grasp their mission. That mission is to teach children how to play a game; how to be a member of a team; how to get along with people; how to respond with grace to pressure situations; and, how to develop their individual skills and abilities to their fullest potential. Our mission as parents, coaches, and leaders in any venue is to help our people prepare to compete effectively and to put them in a position to be winners.

Competition is a vital part of life in social organizations and it is a vital part of life in the natural world. Winning, also, is a worthwhile goal of competition, once we come to understand what winning truly means. Again, the problem is with neither competition nor winning. The problem is with losing. We have attached an unfortunate social stigma to losing.

Losing, itself, is not a bad thing. Think about it for a moment. We sit down to play a table game or a game of cards with friends. When the game is over, one person or one set of partners has won the game and all others have lost. Were the winners the only individuals that enjoyed themselves? No, almost always, nearly everyone had fun. Is the winner the only person who walked away with his or her dignity intact? No, each participant retains his or her dignity. Losing is not the problem.

The real problem is that we confuse losing with being a loser. The two are not the same at all.

On the playing field of the African veldt or in wild America, losing can have dire consequences for what one loses in this game is life itself. In the socio-economic world of modern men and women it is rare that losing has anything but a temporary consequence. Losing is a natural part of playing the game, of participating in life.

The only time losing becomes truly a bad thing is when it becomes pathological; when the person becomes a loser. Losers are people who no longer play the game to win; therefore, they no longer give the game their best effort. They become so afraid of losing that they stop competing altogether or they develop strategies that are risk-avoidance rather than winning strategies. When one stops competing, it is no longer possible to win and there is little joy left in the competition—little joy in living.

Winning is everything in life, once we truly understand what winning means. Winning does not mean beating someone else and being beaten in a game does not make one a loser. Winners are people that always play to win—they utilize all of their skills and talents to the best of their ability, thus placing themselves in a position to succeed. This is not, by the way, an attempt to rationalize parents, very often fathers, who seem unable to let their kids win the games they play together. Adults, that behave, thusly, have forgotten that their purpose is not to beat their children at games rather it is to teach them how to play so that they give themselves an opportunity to win every game they play. No one wins every game they play. What we want is that children learn how to always give themselves an opportunity to win. When that happens, they do not always win but, more importantly, they never truly lose. We want every effort, to create an opptunity to win—to bring about a positive result, to achieve one's objectives.

Returning to our discussion of Little League and other organized sports, it is our contention that these are wonderful activities for children and the only aspect of these activities that should be abolished is the participation of parents who demonstrate a lack of understanding of the mission.

These activities are wonderful opportunities for children to learn how to cooperate; how to be a team player; how to prepare for competition; how to play and work hard; how to deal with pain, adversity, and disappointment as well as with elation and the thrill of victory, which is nothing more than a sense of achievement and accomplishment. In the process, children have fun and they learn the fundamentals of a game that can bring great enjoyment to them throughout their lifetimes.

Look at the animal world. What do baby animals do for hours every day? They play! Not meaningless or purposeless play but play that prepares them for the rigors and challenges of life as a member of their species. It is through play that they develop the strength and skill necessary to survive. It is in their play that they can practice those skills without the risk of losing, which in the animal kingdom has tragic consequences.

The same is true of our children. We want them to engage in play that prepares them for the challenges of their adult life. The emerging involvement of girls in organized team sports and the proliferation of girls' interscholastic and intercollegiate sports will, I believe, do as much as anything to prepare women for the professional and economic equality they seek. The world is a competitive playing field and the people who know and understand the game, and how to play it, will be the men and women who prosper.

**Actions Speak Loudest**

When I was a child and my father would do something that he did not want me to emulate he would say, "Do as I say, not as I do!" Ignore my behavior and pay attention to my words. Of course, it is not the best advice. Our actions speak a thousand, perhaps a million times louder than our words and we pay much more attention to the behavior of our leaders than to their words.

When your teenage children are learning to drive it is your driving habits rather than your verbal admonishments that serve as the model for their behavior. If you speed with regularity, never come to a complete stop, rarely fasten your seatbelt, you can be virtually certain that your teenager will follow your example. And so it is with your people on the job, whatever your level in the organization. If you want your people to listen to and be guided by your words, be certain that your actions are consistent with the words you speak.

Words mean nothing if they conflict with your behavior. If they are supported by your actions, however, your words become a powerful tool. In the latter case, you exemplify that which we call integrity and integrity is one of the most powerful forces in the world.

One of the reasons so many managers are frustrated with their work force is that they honestly believe they are doing the right thing. "I tell my people how important they are all the time!" one manager professes. "But they still don't want to work and I can't count on them to do a quality job unless I watch them every step of the way."

These managers are partially correct. They do say all the right things! They tell their people how valuable and important they are but the words are hollow and meaningless when they are inconsistent with their behavior and with the environment they provide for their people.

Far more than anything we say, it is the things we do that count. Do we listen to our people and act on what we hear? Do we take a personal interest in them? Do we spend time and money attending to their legitimate needs and interests? Do we single them out for their mistakes? Are we on the prowl for trouble? Do we give people credit and recognition for the things that they accomplish? Do we compensate them fairly for the work they do? Do we penalize our people when our company experiences hard times while people in the executive suite get huge bonuses and stock options? Do our rules and regulations create a stifling environment that makes people feel more like inmates than partners in the enterprise?

If you truly want to know how well you do in these areas, do a self-assessment. Examine your organization from stem to stern and do not be afraid to ask your employees what they think about the organization and its leadership team. Your level of discomfort with the results is in direct proportion to your need to hear what your people have to say. And, yes, I know that if you do this out of the blue it is unlikely that your people will be as forthcoming as you need them to be. The solution to this is to seek the help of an objective third party. Hire a consultant or, if you are truly brave, ask the members of your supply chain to help with this process.

**Positive Reinforcement and Encouragement**

When a child learns to walk he or she receives much praise and encouragement.

"Come on! You can do it! Come to Daddy! Atta girl!"

And when they toddle into your waiting arms they are hugged and kissed and tossed into the air and then hugged again. They experience the thrill of accomplishment, the thrill of victory. The child's natural desire to walk, itself a powerful force, is strengthened and fostered by the encouragement and by the reward of the positive attention they receive. When they fall down, we dust them off, hug them, and encourage them to try again.

Imagine the result if the parents' reaction was different.

"Be careful now! Don't fall! Watch out! Don't hurt yourself!"

Or, "let's not try that now, you might hurt yourself!"

The former parent concentrates only on the effort and the achievement while the latter concentrates on the risk of failure. Learning to walk requires a good deal of falling down. It is a necessary part of the process of learning and with each fall the child's brain makes microscopic adjustments in the neuromuscular system that helps improve balance, until walking becomes a learned, autonomous, unconscious activity. During this process we do not worry about falling down at all, even when it results in a few bumps and bruises. And, we do everything we can, such as removing obstacles to reduce the chances of injury, to reduce the consequences of the mistakes children make when striving to learn.

As children grow, the learning process does not change but our attitudes undergo radical change. We become increasingly intolerant of failure and seem to totally disregard the vital role that mistakes plays in learning. Remember that mistakes are not failures at all rather they are learning opportunities.

Our educational system is equally guilty. We expose the child to the material that we wish her to learn, sometimes imaginatively and sometimes boringly. Then, when we think she has had enough, we test her. What is the purpose of the test? Is it to see who needs more attention and to gage how much progress each child is making? We may tell ourselves that this is our motive but look at our actions. We punish the child for her mistakes by counting them against her at the end of the grading period. At the end of the semester the child may know the material as well as anyone in her class, she may even know it better but her grade will be lower because she made more mistakes along the way. The system is set up, it seems, to give the greatest rewards to the child who learns the material most quickly. What we should reward is only the achievement of having reached the objective.

Compare two children learning to ride a bicycle. One hops on the bike and takes off. The second child falls repeatedly over a period of several days until their neuromuscular system catches on. In three weeks the latter child's bumps and bruises are long forgotten and both children derive equal enjoyment from their ability to ride. That one child took a little longer to learn is irrelevant in the final analysis.

By the time many of us reach adulthood, we have been taught to avoid failure, to think of it as something to be feared.

Individuals who are able to overcome this "risk avoidance" pressure are usually successful at whatever goals they seek. They achieve because they do not think of their mistakes as failures. In fact, they do not even use the word "failure." On the contrary, each mistake or setback brings them closer to achievement—each unacceptable outcome provides an opportunity to learn and to adapt and adjust.

We should eliminate the word "failure" from our vocabulary. Similarly, I have often believed that we should stop using the term "home work" in schools and, instead, call it practice. As students practice, we use their mistakes as a way to focus our attention where they most need the help. We want to teach them that mistakes are learning opportunities rather than something that will be counted against them at the end of a semester or grading period.

Organizations that encourage people to extend themselves, that remove obstacles, minimize the consequences of mistakes, that teach people not to fear failure but to learn from mistakes are almost always high-performing organizations. If the leadership of both our educational and business organizations would dedicate itself to removing this fear—our obsession with failure—the results would be astonishing.

Fear, like hate, is a debilitating emotion and fear of failure is a virtual guarantee of mediocrity. Eliminate the fear of failure and you will see revolutionary change in the vitality of your organization and in its productivity.

Pay attention to honest effort, good tries, noble attempts, near misses. Reward, applaud and celebrate effort and enthusiasm, and wild ideas. Make people throughout your organization feel like winners even when they fall short of their objective. Teach them to learn from their mistakes, to reach out, to extend the boundaries of their vision; teach them to shoot for the stars.

**Do More than Mentor, Sponsor!**

The key is to let your people know that your mission is to help them win, to help them succeed:

- Be there for them,
- Fight for them,
- Go to bat for them,
- Stick your neck out for them,
- Raise your expectations of them,
- Demand the best from them,
- Give your best to them,
- Share all the credit with them,
- Take the heat for them,
- Accept responsibility for their mistakes, and
- Smile at them.

Make them feel as though they are the most important resource in the entire organization, like they are partners in the enterprise. Give them a sense of ownership and teach them how to take pride in that ownership.

People respond differently to changes. Watch your people and be alert to signs of stress. Respond by counseling, trying to help the person. It is amazing how much your simple interest will help.

Do all of these things and you will have people who are motivated to do their best and give fully of themselves. Imagine for just a moment how different things would be if this description fit your organization.

A highly motivated workforce can happen. There are numerous businesses that bear witness to this fact. What distinguishes these organizations from the rest is positive leadership; leaders that make their people feel important. Motivation is not something leaders give to their people. Motivation is something that flows from within committed men and women who care about and believe in the mission of the enterprise and who trust its leadership.

# PART III

# THINGS YOU CAN DO!

The key to leadership is action! Our discussion of leadership will be meaningless unless we offer specific suggestions for action strategies that can be implemented immediately. Things you can do that will have a dramatic impact on your life and on the world around you.

Each of these things is not only possible they are imminently doable. All they require is a willing participant who will open his or her heart to the possibilities and will act and act now!

Our discussion will address strategies for the full spectrum of our lives to include home, the community, and the workplace. This list of strategies is not intended to be exhaustive. Our purpose is to get you started, to serve as an ignition system. The list is as long as your imagination, so use your imagination and add to the list continually.

## *nine*
## ACTION PLANS AND PROPOSALS

The process of preparing action plans and action proposals is crucial to effective positive leadership. But what do we mean? What is an action plan and how does it differ from an action proposal? What purpose do they serve and to whom are they directed?

**ACTION PLANS**

Action plans are the essence of simplicity. An action plan is the statement of a specific objective and a listing, in sequence, of the actions you intend to take to achieve your objective. An action plan can fit on an index card or, for that matter, on the back of a business card. On the other hand, it can be a ten, twenty or even a one hundred page document according to the scope and complexity of the contemplated action.

An action plan is what you need when you are prepared and able to take action on your own initiative or when you are the decision maker. If you are the only actor it can be brief. If the contemplated action requires the coordinated participation of other members of your team then the action plan may require more detailed descriptions and explanations. However long it may be, it remains a simple statement of objectives and the specific actions (steps, behaviors, tasks, etc.) that are to be implemented.

It is vital that the action plan also stipulates the expected results or outcomes along with some discussion as to the manner in which the results will be measured or interpreted. Action plans are meaningless unless they lead to action and action is meaningless unless it is purposeful and produces measurable outcomes.

Some action plans may require a brief statement about the overall mission or purpose. Others, particularly if they are action plans involving only one individual, may not. In the latter case, it is assumed that the mission is clearly envisioned in the mind of the actor and requires no articulation. When multiple personalities are involved it is best not to make assumptions with respect to the clarity of one's mission and more articulation is desirable.

An action plan establishes a framework for accountability so that it can be evaluated both in terms of the efficiency (how well the plan was implemented) and effectiveness (were the desired results achieved.)

Any time you are faced with a challenge, think it through and prepare and implement an action plan.

## ACTION PROPOSALS

Action proposals are nothing more than a special type of action plan for situations in which you are unable to act unilaterally or, when you lack the authority to act. In these situations your response to the challenge depends on your ability to influence other people and convince them that the action you propose is necessary and beneficial. Hence action proposals require more articulation and all major assumptions must be identified at the outset.

The well-conceived action proposal should include:

1. A statement of the overall mission or purpose;
2. A set of specific action objectives;
3. A description of how and why the proposed actions will effectively serve the mission or purpose;
4. The cost of the action compared to the perceived benefits;

5. The method by which results will be measured and interpreted; and,
6. A call for action.

Again the breadth and scope of the proposal depends on the size and complexity of the operation and the number of people involved. Action proposals are not comprehensive strategic plans, however, and they need not fill notebooks. The proposal should be sufficiently brief that the decision maker can read it and act quickly. Prepare an action proposal in a way that makes it easy for the decision maker to say yes or no!

*ten*

# ACTION STRATEGIES FOR HOME, FAMILY, AND COMMUNITY

**Exercise your mind, body, and self esteem.**
   Actions:
   <u>Implement an exercise program to get your body in shape</u>. Do it at home or away from home. Walk, exercise, play tennis or basketball, ride a real or stationary bicycle, join a health club or the YMCA or YWCA, take aerobic classes, join the walkers' club at your nearest shopping mall. Do not overdo it! Start slowly and build up to a daily regimen that works for you, but make a commitment and stick to it. You will feel better, have more energy, stamina, and more enthusiasm for life and be less susceptible to depression.

   <u>Initiate a reading program</u>. Set aside at least fifteen to twenty minutes a day, at a time that works well for you, to read something educational or inspirational beyond the local newspaper. Feel free to vary the material you read according to your interests and activities and according to your job requirements. It will expand your mind and your imagination, introduce you to new ideas, broaden your vocabulary and, if you are reading positive, uplifting material it will improve your positive outlook and inspire you to live your life more fully.

    <u>Commence a serious regimen for your self esteem</u>. Listen to motivational tapes. Smile and talk to yourself in the mirror. Read motivational books. Keep a diary of your innermost thoughts and feelings as you strive to build a positive self-concept. Begin to think of yourself as a giving person and start doing things for other people. Nothing makes us feel better about ourselves than to receive positive feedback from the people in our lives; and nothing generates positive feedback from the people in our lives more than doing things to help those people feel good about themselves. Share yourself with the people about whom you care! These things you do for yourself, but not only for yourself. The best way to enhance your contribution to your family, your job, and community is to take good care of yourself. You are important to the people in your life. They care about you and they need you. Take good care of yourself for their sake as well as for your own sake. Go on a sensible diet, not a fad diet; take a vitamin and mineral supplement. If you are unhappy with your appearance, do something about it. Get a new hair style; dress differently; try a different style of eyeglasses.

   Begin to look at yourself through different eyes. When you look at yourself through the eyes of someone who feels good about themselves you can begin to see the warmth and the friendliness in your face, especially if you are smiling. Discard the idea that you have to look like a movie star; very few people possess that type of good looks. Think instead of all the friendly and interesting people you know. Think about their faces and their appearance. How do you perceive them? You enjoy seeing them because they are warm and friendly people and the various characteristics of their appearance are distinguishing. What draws you to them are not their facial or physical beauty, but their warmth and friendliness, their openness and their genuine concern for you. Think of yourself as this type of person and very soon you will begin to see that type of person when you look and smile at yourself in the mirror.

   <u>Think positive, life-affirming thoughts as often as possible</u>. Fill your mind with positive thoughts and purge yourself of as many negative thoughts and feelings as possible. Count your blessings. Do not be discouraged when negative thoughts keep cropping up. They are

normal for all human beings. Think of it as weeding the garden. The more you pull the weeds the more the flowers flourish, yet the weeds keep coming. It is a never-ending job. Once you have cleared the garden a few times, however, the weed growth begins to diminish. So, too, will it be with your negative feelings and thoughts.

<u>Change the way you respond to people</u>. When someone asks how you are doing, how do you respond? Try something new the next time someone asks. Say: "Better than I have in a long time!" If they want to hear more you can say: "I have been working to develop a positive attitude and it has given me a whole new outlook on life." You do not have to say any more than this but be sure to smile when you say it. If people want to know more then don't be shy. Share your gift of positive living with them and you will feel even better about yourself. Do not worry as you would in the past, about being embarrassed.

When you meet other people, do not push your ideas on them but reach out to them in a totally different way. Give them your attention, after all your attention is one of the greatest gifts you can give to another human being. Listen to them and hear what they are saying. Ask relevant questions that demonstrate that you are listening. Give them positive feedback and encouragement at every opportunity without preaching and without talking about yourself. Do not talk about yourself at all unless they ask. As you truly listen to others and give them your attention, fully, you are making them feel like the most important person in the world, at that moment, and they will choose to spend more time with you than they may have ever done in the past. Become an empathic listener.

Do a self-assessment exercise such as we discussed in Chapter Four. Rejoice in and celebrate the positive things in your life and convert the things about which you are unhappy to action strategies for change.

**Re-evaluate your use of time.**

<u>Keep track, for a week, of the things you do each day</u> and how much time they require. Make a commitment to convert your unproductive, passive leisure time to constructive activities that will make

you feel good about yourself. Remember our discussion about leisure time. Idle time may bring the illusion of enjoyment but true joy comes from doing positive things.

<u>Reduce passive activities, to start, by an hour per day</u> and devote that time to doing something positive. Cut back on the amount of time you spend watching television. If you are a TV addict, start gradually and reduce the number of shows you watch by eliminating your least favorite. If necessary, list all of the shows you watch and rate them for their importance. Eliminate the shows that rank lowest on your list and replace them with a constructive activity.

<u>Think about how materialistic you are</u>. Most of us have grown up with the idea that success is measured by our acquisition of material possessions. There is nothing inherently wrong with wanting nice things. Nice things, however, do not bring happiness and, in fact, they have nothing to do with happiness. Possessions can actually become an impediment to happiness because we frequently get so wrapped up in our possessions that we forget about the things that are truly important in our lives and that lead to real joy. Do you need nice things? Where do material possessions rank in your life when compared to the people in your life? Does your behavior reflect those priorities or do you find yourself sacrificing time with your spouse, children, friends, or with yourself to achieve materialistic goals and objectives?

What are the things you really need in your life to be happy and what are you willing to trade for them? Far too many Americans seem captivated by material things to the exclusion of all else. They may not do so consciously but they constantly sacrifice their family life, their relationship with their spouse and children to acquire a nice house in a nice neighborhood with two nice cars and all of the other trappings that fit their image of affluent America. Along the way, their marriage turns sour and their children grow apart from them and they find themselves with money to spare but have no one with whom it can be shared. Their lives are empty. Where do these things fall on your priority list? What is the focus of your attention? What is your mission?

Think about the things you really need to be happy in life and they almost always come down to people. Re-think the way you live your life to put the people who are close to you back at the top of your priority list. People create joy and happiness in life, money does not. Money may reduce discomfort or dissatisfaction but it truly cannot bring happiness. Most people who are willing to work hard and give of themselves—who are positive leaders—can have both if their priorities are in the right place. Concentrate your energies on the things that are truly important and you may be surprised at how successful you can be economically. Most of all, accept the fact that you deserve happiness. If life sometimes seems overwhelming, do not be alarmed. We all feel that way at times. If, however, life seems overwhelming most of the time, get help for yourself. You deserve better and you can have better. Remember that you are a child of God and that nothing that can happen to you in life at the hands of man or nature can diminish your worth and value as a human being.

**Family**

<u>Give of yourself to your family</u>. There are very few things in life that can bring as much joy as a happy family. Devote yourself to your family. There are many people in the world who have a limited number of personal possessions but yet experience the daily joy of being alive because of their family. Put your family at the top of your priority list and make a commitment to family.

Families mean children and our children deserve the absolute best that we have to offer. What our children want and need are not nice things that we can buy for them. There are few possessions that add real meaning to their lives. What our children require are loving, giving, caring, sharing, supportive parents who spend time with them. Parents who pay attention to them, teach them, listen to them, hold out expectations for them, protect them, set boundaries for them, and demand discipline of them. These things are your responsibility. Your children need you to be there for them, to be strong for them. They need the best that you have to offer. Here are just a few things you can do.

Read to your children. Parents who begin reading to their children when they are infants not only establish a pattern of literacy but also create strong emotional bonds. Think about the process of reading. It involves spending time with your children in an activity that is emotionally, physically, and intellectually intimate. We hold them on our lap, cuddle up next to them in an easy chair or in bed; we engage their imaginations; the sound of our voice becomes imprinted in their hearts and minds and memories; we share laughter, adventure, and an entire range of emotions.

Play with your children. Get down on the floor and play with them; enter their world. Encourage their imaginations and let them explore new adventures while teaching them that they are safe and secure in your arms. Teach them not to be afraid.

Find time each day. Spend time with your children to make them feel special even if it is only a few moments. Hold them in your lap, have a snack with them, sit down to a meal with them, talk to them. Ask about their day and then truly listen to what they have to say. Take time to understand the things that are going on in their lives. Teach them that they can share victories and losses, sadness and joy, fears and aspirations with you. Listen empathically. Listening empathically does not require that one give advice. Refrain from giving advice until we are sure advice is really needed. Often, our children just need us to listen not only to what they did but how they felt.

Do family things. Go on outings, play games, help with their homework, do house or yard work together, take vacations together. Tell them how special they are and tell them how much you love them. Tell them stories about when they were little. Tell them stories about you when you were a child. Kid around with them and laugh with them, especially when they tease you. Teach them how to laugh at themselves by laughing at yourself.

Give your children the structure of discipline. Set clear guidelines and expectations. Talk about values and about right and wrong. Do not be afraid to say no and do not be talked into something you know in your heart isn't right. If your children throw a tantrum or keep begging for things, be strong for them and stand your ground. Such tantrums truly are a test that our children give to us and it is important that we pass those tests. Tantrums are an inappropriate attempt on the part of the child to gain control over their environment. Teach them appropriate ways to gain control over their lives. There is security in clear and definitive boundaries. They need you to teach them that they cannot win those types of battles. Teach them how to handle disappointment.

<u>Teach them responsibility</u>. Hold them accountable for their actions. Do not shield your children from the natural consequences of their behavior. Do not bail them out or protect them when they misbehave, but do not abandon them either. Teach them how to admit their mistakes and to learn from them. Teach them by example, by honestly admitting your own mistakes. Teach them that mistakes are a natural part of learning, growing, and reaching for ever-higher goals and expectations. Be there for your children. Help them learn that even when they must stand alone that they are never truly alone; that we are with them always even in their moments of despair.

<u>Set a good example for your children</u>. Lead the kind of life you want them to have. Do not use the "Do as I say, not as I do!" approach. Live your values and explain them along the way. The way they observe you living your life provides a far more powerful model than anything you can say. If your life is centered around things, if you look for ways to avoid hard work, if your behavior is illegal or immoral, if your values are shallow and superficial; these are the traits your children will emulate. If, however, you embrace life with a positive spirit and attitude you are providing a model that will sustain them throughout their entire life, long after you are gone.

<u>Get involved with your children</u>. Visit them at school, volunteer to accompany their class on field trips. Participate in Girl Scouts or Boy Scouts, 4-H, Little League, youth soccer, dance or music classes, etc. Support their teachers and coaches and recognize that these and the other professionals who come into their lives are your partners. Avoid creating scenarios in which your children find themselves in the middle of opposing forces.

<u>Hug your children at every opportunity</u>, both physically and emotionally and do not stop just because they get to be a certain age. Kiss

them and smile at them.  Remember that the children who are hardest to love are the ones who need it the most.  Remember that hugs, kisses and smiles are life-affirming to both the giver and the receiver.  Best of all, they cost absolutely nothing.  They are free of charge and they are available in infinite quantity.

<u>Avoid the pitfalls of affluence</u>.  One of the most difficult things in all of parenthood is to raise your children in affluence.  Parents who shower their children with material gifts and possessions, things that have not been earned by the child's hard work and accomplishments, creates an entitlement personality.  Such personalities lead to selfish, empty, and unhappy lives. Teach them that affluence is a blessing that can be enjoyed but that it did not come free of charge.

<u>Teach your children to give of themselves</u>.  It truly is better to give than to receive and there are few things in life that create as much joy as a generous heart.  Teach them also that giving of one's self sometimes requires that we allow others to give to us.  Help them learn the art of gracious acceptance of the gifts of others.  Help them develop an abundance mentality in which there is always enough to go around. Help them learn that being able to delight in the joys and successes of other people is a precious gift.

As your children get older, peer pressure will become a powerful force in their lives and unless you have done your job of preparing your children well, that peer pressure can literally alter the direction of your child's life.

Give your children the best education possible but do not choose a school as a way to protect them from the real world. The answer is to share with them the values they need so that they can live successfully in the real world.  Teach them how to socialize with their peers but give them the strength of character they will need to extricate themselves when the group goes too far. Kids in possession of a healthy self-esteem and a clear value system are capable of making good decisions in even the most challenging of circumstances. On many occasions, my children called to get permission to do something when I could tell by the sound of their voice that they wanted me to say no. That is just one way you can help your children make good decisions.

<u>Let them do it</u>. Do not do it for your children if they can do it for themselves. We learn by doing and parents that insist on doing everything for their children only create dependencies. Teach your children to be strong and independent rather than weak and dependent. Remember that spilled milk is easier to clean up than the mess we create when we raise children who cannot stand alone. Also remember that being able to stand alone is not being alone.

<u>Remember what it was like when you were a child</u>. Do not expect perfection from your children and do not expect it from yourself. It is inevitable that you will make mistakes with your children, all parents do. But children are remarkably resilient creatures and they will survive your mistakes as long as you do your best to love and cherish them. Remember that, like you, they too are a child of God.

**Spouse or Lover**

Whether you are a man or a woman, your job is to give of yourself; to wish happiness for your partner and then to do whatever you can to make it happen. This is your mission in life, to be a giver rather than a taker. If you give of yourself fully, it is inevitable that your partner will give to you as well.

<u>Be your partner's best friend</u>. Be his or her cheerleader, moral support, and advocate as well as lover and companion. Take joy in his or her success in life because they are your successes as well. Pull for them to be fulfilled in life and to be self-actualized. Do all these things and your partner will return them in full measure. It may not seem so at first, but by giving of yourself you are enriching your partner's self-esteem. The healthier your spouse or lover's ego the more he or she is able to give. Remember that "what goes around, comes around."

<u>Make your partner feel that they are important</u> and that what they do and say is also important. Listen to them and communicate honestly. Let them know that they can count on you for honest feedback and that they need not be embarrassed because of their imperfections. The more you give and the more you share, the more you shall receive in return.

Give fully of yourself sexually and learn what makes your partner happy. Strive to give them pleasure and you will learn the magical secret of sexual fulfillment. The more you give of yourself the more they will give in return. When both partners strive equally to give the other pleasure, joyfully, both will experience one of our Creator's greatest gifts. The secret is, once again, giving. The more we give, the more we receive. It is truly a prescription for life.

When barriers are erected between you and your partner, break them down. Talk to one another no matter how difficult it seems. If you are unable to say it out loud, write a letter. If the barriers loom too large, seek help from a trained professional. Remember that the relationship is more important than anything you possess. It is more important than the house, the cars; it is more important than anything but your self-esteem. Remember that your children are an inherent part of the relationship and not something separate and apart.

The relationship must always enhance the self to be healthy. If, at any time, the relationship seems to require that one partner give up his or her identity then the relationship is unhealthy. Healthy relationships demand the absolute commitment to the well-being of one's partner. Each must be devoted to the other in this respect. Anything short of this is selfishness and selfishness is the destructive force at the root of much of the trouble in not only our relationships but also in our society.

Yes, there will be inevitable conflicts and differences of opinion. Both partners will have strengths and weaknesses and the sharing will, at times, be unequal. Neither has a right to expect perfection but both have the right to expect the best of one another. When problems arise, do not keep score of who did what to whom or who owes what. Sacrifice your self esteem for no one because by doing so you weaken both you and the quality of your relationships.

Help each other. Share responsibilities. Talk about the personal goals and expectations of each and divvy up responsibilities according to those goals and expectations. When both partners have careers, it is vital that the partners understand that a team effort is required at home. Both partners must share equally with the responsibilities of childcare and home. Remember that the best marriages and the healthiest children come from marriages that are distinguished by full partnership.

Sharing a life together can be the single greatest joy in all of life. It is greater than anything money can buy and it is worth any sacrifice. It is the source of strength that can sustain each partner through all of the ups and downs of life and that will allow you to delight in your life, no matter what challenges life brings to bear. When we see what is happening throughout our society, with the divorce rate and the disintegration of so many families, it is a sad thing. It is a symptom of our systemic selfishness. Many men and women make poor decisions when selecting their mate, relying on superficial criteria. Then, we fail to give fully of ourselves in the effort to make the relationship work.

We place our value in things that are, at their core, meaningless. We want nice things: a beautiful house in a prestigious neighborhood, expensive furniture, nice cars, flashy toys, and nice vacations. Some of us consider it imperative that they belong to the most exclusive country clubs. We want all we can get, yet none of these things lead to joy and happiness. They are not inherently bad things but it is the quest for their acquisition that can lead to disillusionment and unhappiness. The only joy in life comes through our relationships with our Creator, however we individually may choose to view the Creation, and with the people whom we love and cherish. Things have meaning only within the context of our relationships with people and a life that has been dominated by the desire for material things is destined for heartbreak.

Rethink your values. Examine the focus of your time and energy. If that focus is on material things rather than on the people in your life then it is time for a radical realignment. Remember, always, that people are more important than things. If you refocus that attention on your spouse, your children, your family, and friends you will rediscover absolute joy in your life.

## In Your Community

How much time and energy one devotes to one's community will vary greatly according to the time of one's life. What is important is that we each acknowledge a responsibility to our community, to society, and to the world as a whole. Remember to think about things in the context of our most basic values:

1. That every human being on the face of the Earth is a child of God and deserves our respect and concern

2. That the universe is God's gift to us

We have an unyielding obligation to cherish life and the universe. Everything we do must be judged in this context: Does it or does it not affirm life? We must:

- Respect all human beings
- Reject racism
- Conserve and protect the Earth's resources:
  - Conserve energy
  - Reduce solid waste
  - Protect the environment
  - Practice ecological consumerism (make purchasing decisions on the basis of a product's environmental equation)
- Participate in our own governance at the local, state and federal level by:
  - Voting
  - Paying taxes
  - Serving our country when called upon
  - Serving on jury duty when called
  - Answering census questionnaires
- Help our neighbors
- Take care of our property
- Support the less fortunate with our energy, compassion, time, and money
- Support our economy by doing our job to the best of our ability
- Support our local educational systems, both public and private
- Give something back to our community

None of us can afford to live in isolation or to abdicate responsibility for the world and its challenges. Whether we accept it or not, the problems of the world will have an impact on our lives and on the lives of our loved ones. None of the world's problems can be effectively resolved without the help of each of us. None of us are insignificant and each effort on the part of every individual makes a difference. Remember the words of Jane Goodall,

*The most important thing people can do for the future of the world is to realize that what they do matters.*

Every child that grows up hungry, angry, ignorant, and estranged from the mainstream of our society, threatens the safety and quality of life of the entire community. These children are our responsibility and the sooner we acknowledge that responsibility the better our chances of making a positive impact. If every gainfully employed man or woman would reach back to help one disadvantaged child, there would not be enough disadvantaged children to go around.

Most of us look out at the immense problems in the world and feel overwhelmed and powerless. This is a normal human feeling but it is just that—a feeling. We are not powerless and we need not feel overwhelmed. We have the power to make a difference if only we will accept responsibility for the world around us—if only we will take the lead.

Give of yourself fully. Take on a cause or a pet program and donate both time and money. Make it a family affair and select something that you, your spouse, and children can do together. If you are single, select a project that you and your friends can share.

Former President George H.W. Bush's 1988 campaign strategy of promoting "a thousand points of light" may or may not have been successful but it was an important acknowledgement that our government cannot solve all of our problems. In fact, just the opposite is the case. More often than not our government tends to create more problems than it solves. The best solutions to our problems rest in the hands of individual men and women acting in concert and on principle. You can make a difference. More importantly, you must make a difference!

## ACTION STRATEGIES – AT WORK

### When You Are the Employee

Give your best effort all of the time. Take pride in the work you do regardless of how menial or sophisticated. Focus your mind and your energies at all times on the end-customer who will derive benefit from that which you do whether that is someone outside of your organization or within. Accept as your mission the responsibility for giving that customer the best product or service possible given the resources with which you are provided.

Value your job as an opportunity to contribute something of value to society. Each and every job is part of the fabric that is our socio-economic system. As complicated and remote as it may seem, each job done well, contributes value to the system. Recall the reference to J.D. Salinger's book Franny and Zooey and "do it for the fat lady." Seymour's "fat lady" was a symbolic representation of Jesus Christ. The point Seymour Glass wished to make for his younger siblings was that they should always do and look their best for Christ and everything He represents. Doing so adds an element of beauty to the world. The universe may be vast and complicated but the contributions of individual men and women are still the primary determinant of the overall quality of life for all members of a society.

Think in terms of primitive man's early days when society was the extended family or tribe. No matter how primitive the community, a clear division of labor existed in which all participants were expected to contribute according their talents and abilities. The whole tribe derived benefit from a job well done and the whole tribe suffered if it was done poorly. Although modern society is complex, things have not changed all that much. What you do is still important to the welfare of the community and it is your responsibility to do it to the best of your ability.

Do not ask "what's in it for me?" Do not take the attitude that I will do it only when I'm certain of the reward. Do it for the customer who will benefit, whether internal or external. Do it for the community that depends on everyone to do his or her best; do it for your own pride and self esteem.

Put your trust in your employer. Yes, there is risk that an employer may take advantage of you, that you may be exploited. There is risk in all of life. Someone has to break the cycle of mistrust, however, so why not let it be you? And, do not be afraid to ask management to put its trust in you. If you find that your employer does not deserve your trust, do something about it even if that means finding a better job. Most of the time, however, we can make our current job better.

Do not complain about things you Do not like or that make it more difficult to do your job. Instead, propose a positive alternative. Think through the issue and talk to other people who view the problem from a range of perspectives. Then prepare a brief but simple action proposal and submit it to the appropriate authorities. Do not worry about whether or not it will be approved. Many of your suggestions will be ignored; some, however, will be accepted. Some will be filed away for future reference and will re-surface when the time is ripe. Other proposals will be scorned; and, some will spark a germ of an idea in the mind of someone else and will be a catalyst for change.

Something else will happen, as well, as you develop a pattern of preparing action proposals. If your ideas are positive and practical you will acquire a reputation as a problem-solver, as a leader, and as an employee to be listened to and respected. Most important of all, the customer whom you serve will derive real benefit. As this happens, you will also earn the respect of your peers who will view you as an individual who can get management to take notice. As a result, people will begin to recognize your leadership. Never under-estimate the power of committed men and women. They can and do change the world! It happens every day, everywhere. You can too!

Talk to people and listen to them. Smile at them and be friendly. Help people to learn how to do their jobs. Reach out to them. Set a good example. Do not feel compelled to knuckle under to peer-pressure but instead, stand up for your values and principles.

<u>Be a hero</u>. When we were children we pretended to be heroes who would display our courage under even the most trying and dangerous circumstances. The workforce presents opportunities for heroism, daily, and the world needs you every bit as desperately today as in wartime. And, the benefit to be derived from your leadership is vital to our society. So go ahead! Be a hero! The worst thing that can happen to you as a result of your courage is that a few individuals with little minds and weak spines may make snide remarks. They are inconsequential. It is heroes that the world needs so earnestly.

Work hard, be honest, stay late, volunteer for the tough assignments, innovate, streamline, establish a new standard, communicate with management, demonstrate your loyalty, say what needs to be said even in the face of danger. Have strength and courage. Dedicate yourself to doing the best job you can and expect—even demand—the same from those around you. Our entire society, our way of life, is threatened by a lack of commitment and heroism; by the unwillingness of men and women to stand up for what is right and to give unselfishly of their talents and skills. You can make a difference! It is your duty to yourself, to your children, and to your children's children. It is also your duty to your sense of honor. It is this kind of effort and courage that made America the beacon of hope for the world and it is this type of courage and effort that will revitalize and re-energize our nation, today and in the future.

**When You Are the Boss**

<u>Accept that your most important resource is your people</u>. However imperfect they may seem and however many problems they may have caused they have more than enough potential to help your department succeed.

They are your people. You either selected them or accepted them because they were thought to have the ability to do the job. Now they are your people and you are responsible for developing their potential. Remember that unless they are incompetent and/or unwilling, it is less expensive to remediate the problems they cause than to replace them. Place your faith and trust in them; elevate your expectations. If you are forced to conclude that your people do not have the potential your department requires, it is your responsibility to do something about it.

<u>Let your people know what the company's objectives</u> are and let them know when it succeeds or fails and how you and they have contributed to that success or failure. Do not withhold data about the company's performance. Remember that knowledge is power. Most employees have an intuitive understanding of what it takes to be profitable and, with a little help from you, to teach them how to understand the numbers, you will likely be surprised at the manner of their response.

One of the best ways to do this is to give them specific information relating to the expectations of your customers.

<u>Let your people know what your department's job is and how it contributes to the success of the business</u>. Also let them know how your department interacts with other departments and how these departments mutually support one another. Make certain your people understand how their jobs fit in the program and how they contribute to the success of the department and to the business as a whole. Identify the internal supply chains that exist for each department. Make sure they understand who exists to serve whom. Who are their internal customers and what are the expectations of these customers?

<u>Whenever possible, help your people set specific goals and objectives</u>. This does not mean setting those expectations for them. Expectations should be as high as possible as long as they are achievable and the more your employees participate in setting those expectations the more powerful they will be. If they do not feel a sense of ownership over the expectations that have been established the

expectations will be less meaningful. Then, measure performance and publish the results. Find something to count. Celebrate all victories.

Let your people know that your job, as their supervisor, is to help them succeed, and then, do your job.

Become a strong advocate. Fight for your people and stand up for them. See that they get the credit when they deserve it.

Take advantage of every opportunity to give positive feedback and recognition. Feedback is not something that should occur on a schedule or on special occasions. Positive feedback should comprise a significant part of what we do, each and every day.

Establish an atmosphere that concerns itself with solving problems not fixing the blame. Allow for mistakes and for failure. Give recognition for a good try. The only people who never make mistakes are those that never accept a challenge and never extend themselves. Recall the adage that says that "unless you fall down once in a while, you are not really skiing." Remember that mistakes are nothing more than wonderful learning opportunities.

Make a commitment to listen. Seek out the ideas and suggestions of your people and act on them. Establish a system of incentives that will encourage more ideas and suggestions. Let people know the outcome of their ideas and suggestions.

Manage on the move, out amongst your employees. Never underestimate the power of your physical presence and the number of opportunities your presence creates. Avoid the ivory tower image.

Operate with an open-door policy. Contrary to popular belief, an open-door policy does not weaken the chain of command. The rule of thumb is that "you can and should listen to anyone, anytime, but avoid taking action until you have heard all sides, gathered the facts, and involve all of the appropriate participants." Schedule times when you are available—otherwise your time will be devoured by circumstances beyond your control and the open-door policy will be a myth. Your people know how busy you are and that there are many demands for your time. When you guarantee time for them it will help them appreciate how precious your time is and how important they are that you are willing to share it with them. Remember that the best open-door policy is the one in which the boss is going out among the people as well as allowing the people to come to the boss.

You will not be able to solve all of their problems but you will establish a positive atmosphere that will be fertile ground for productivity and excellence. Offer structured opportunities through which your employees can communicate with you. Create focus groups, have informal lunch meetings. Invite people to brain-storming sessions.

Handle problems, don't create them. Take action to resolve problem situations and to respond to problem behavior by people, face-to-face, eyeball-to-eyeball. Rather than criticize or punish people, deal with the natural consequences of behavior. Leave personalities out of it as much as possible. Solve problems at the lowest possible level.

Avoid the temptation to legislate solutions to problems. This gets the supervisor off the hook, temporarily, of having to deal with a problem, but it punishes the whole unit or department and it does not address the underlying problem. After all, behaviors are nothing more than symptoms of underlying issues. More often than not, it is the employee's lack of commitment to the mission that is driving undesirable behavior. Do not make the innocent majority suffer for the misdeeds of the few. In these situations, the innocent taste the bitterness of injustice and nothing destroys trust in leadership more than perceived injustice. Use the "few rules theory of leadership."

Rules are the studs, joists, and rafters of bureaucracies. When the behavior of an individual compromises the mission or purpose of an organization, positive leaders go to the source. Positive leaders begin with the assumption that the individual wants to do a good job but has, somehow, been diverted from their purpose. Positive leaders view these events as opportunities to teach and also opportunities to build trust. They begin by reminding themselves of their purpose as a positive leader, which is to help individual men and women be successful.

"Hold on a minute!" you might say. "That is not the outcome we are seeking."

A leader's focus on outcomes, whether desirable or not, shifts the focus away from the individual. Imagine how differently you feel when someone accuses you of doing something wrong, compared to a simple response of surprise that the outcome of the effort was not what we wanted or expected. It changes the entire dynamics of the conversation. Positive leaders have the highest possible expectations of their people and they avoid searching for evil intent.

Inevitably, even in the career of the most positive leader, there will be men and women with the intent to work in the disinterest of their organization. Exemplary leaders are always shocked to discover people of bad character because they expect the best of everyone. When an individual to whom every consideration has been given, proves him or herself as untrustworthy, positive leaders respond with the gavel of certain justice. These leaders respond unhesitatingly and unequivocally. At the moment when the positive leader becomes convinced that an individual can no longer be trusted, the leader's efforts shift immediately from the focus on remediation to one of acting in the best interests of the organization. Rarely are the interests of an organization served by hesitation or vacillation. Positive leaders waste no time and immediately get the individual out of the organization.

Many managers and supervisors feel powerless to address issues of employee performance and behavior because organizations must, out of necessity, protect itself from litigation. The best protection against litigation is not inaction rather it is appropriate and well-documented action.

<u>Learn as many names as possible and smile at the people you encounter.</u> Acknowledge your people as valuable human beings. Treat them with dignity and respect. People do not normally respond

to embarrassment or humiliation. "KAP! Kick Ass Privately" when it is necessary to kick ass at all. Make people feel important. Have a training session for your entire management team to teach them how to make people feel important.

<u>Your integrity and your character are your most important assets</u>. You do not have to be right all the time nor do you need to win all of the battles.

<u>Vent your frustrations and express your doubts only to your peers or to your boss</u>. Even the penultimate leader feels doubt and frustration—after all they are human beings. It is okay to be human. What distinguishes positive leaders from their less effective counterparts is the recognition of their responsibility to put the interests of their organization and its people ahead of their personal interests. They vent their frustrations appropriately. Require the same of your staff. Encourage them to vent their frustrations to you. Once a policy is made by management, Do not burden your staff with your disagreement or disenchantment with that policy. Carry out the policy with the same positive enthusiasm you would display if it were your pet project or idea. If you are a strong advocate, as you well should be you will have given testimony of your opinion in the policy formation process. In dealing with your staff, encourage them to express their honest opinion about every topic until such time as a decision is made. Once the decision is made, expect them to support it enthusiastically.

<u>Let your people know that you trust them to do their job</u>, to produce results, to meet deadlines, to achieve objectives. Then let them do their jobs. Do not look over their shoulder until they have missed their deadlines. Give them honest feedback about their results. Remember that trust is one of the most important characteristics of a successful organization. Work hard to earn their trust in you.

<u>You are the leader – so lead</u>! Be proactive! Be decisive! Accept responsibility! Keep an eye on the future!

Build teamwork! Talk to your people about the role you want them to play and about its importance to the organization. See that they get recognition for that contribution and that they get to share in victories as a full member of the team. Intermix individual performance goals with team goals. If an individual's performance holds the team back, involve the team in the resolution.

Insist on the facts! Know your department inside and out. Know what it produces and how much it costs to produce it. Do not be afraid of the facts. They can be a powerful tool to get things done and the more you and your people know about your operation the better your outcomes.

Teach your people to accept responsibility for their jobs! When they come to you with problems or questions, use it as an opportunity to teach them how to think for themselves. Good leaders resist the temptation, when the employee is stuck on a problem, to take over and solve it. The goal is not to solve the problem and show how smart you are; the goal is to help the employee solve the problem and to teach them how smart he or she can be. Ask them what they think. They may be extremely reluctant to share their ideas with you for fear of looking stupid, but ninety percent of the time they will have an idea that may lead to a solution.

"Give a man a fish and you feed him for the day. Teach him how to fish and you feed him for a lifetime!"

Teach your people how to be strong and independent rather than weak and dependent! Many supervisors think it necessary to keep their staff dependent on them when, in fact, this only weakens the organization. Effective supervisors are constantly working to help their staff become independent within the scope of their jobs. It is only when we have taught people how to be independent that we can shift our focus to interdependence.

Expect your people to be the best and expect your department to be the best. Make certain that your expectations are communicated to everyone. There is substantial evidence to support that most people will strive to live up to or down to the expectations of their leaders. There are very few people in the world who want to be a loser. People will follow a leader with a winning attitude. Leaders who believe their people are winners and who expect them to win, consistently produce winning teams.

<u>Do not make threats, make promises</u>. And do not make promises you cannot keep or that you do not intend to keep. Threats are negative strategies by people who usually have no power to act. They serve only to diminish a leader's credibility. Unfulfilled promises also damage credibility. Once you lose your credibility your people begin to lose respect for you. A leader without the respect of his or her people is doomed to mediocrity at the very best!

<u>When confronted with problems take action to solve them</u>. When you have no authority to act, prepare an plan of action in the form of an action proposal and present it to someone who does have authority. Give them enough information and sufficient options that they need only answer yes or no! There is never an excuse for inaction unless the problem is found not to be a real problem.

<u>Deal with people in terms of their and your intelligent self-interest</u>. Make decisions and take risks! Be patient and tolerant, set standards for others that represent their capabilities, not yours. Keep communication channels clear and rise above emotional barriers. Above all, accept responsibility for everything that happens in your department. But remember that responsibility and blame are not synonymous. In fact, forget about blame. Blame is a negative activity that contributes nothing to progress. Contrary to conventional thinking, identifying causes and sources of problems is not the equivalent of blame. Focusing on causes and sources of problems is a focus on outcomes whereas a focus on blame is a focus on the imperfections of our people.

<u>Set productivity goals that can be met by the majority of people</u> in the workforce rather than by only a select few. Better yet, let your

people establish their own productivity goals. The object is to set them high enough to generate pride in achievement, but low enough that the majority begin to feel like winners. Publish those objectives for the world to see and post the results just as prominently. Let the results speak for themselves. With each victory, raise the level of your expectations.

Begin the process of dismantling the bureaucracy. Try to find one rule a month that can be abolished. The more freedom you give your people the more responsibility you have a right to expect. The more responsibility people have the greater their sense of ownership. Establish the ritual of inviting your people to nominate one rule a month for the scrap pile. You will also find this is an effective way to reduce your costs as each rule places an enforcement burden on the enterprise. Involving your people in this process contributes to high morale.

Create an integrated performance management system that works very much like the quality systems involved in your production process. Create a real-time system that involves people in the development of expectations; that taps their knowledge within the context of a learning organization; that adapts continuously with the dynamic business environment; that insures that people have ongoing positive feedback on their performance and outcomes; that gives people access to as much meaningful information as possible; and, that encourages an ownership mentality. Integrated performance management systems give people a real sense that they have an element of control over their situations and outcomes. Such systems are an incredibly powerful tool.

The list can go on and on. Build on this list! Use it as a springboard. We have tried to leave room with each of these strategies for you to flesh them out with greater specificity relative to your organization and industry. Personalize them; tailor them to your individual tastes and preferences but, whatever, do something! Act!

Remember that anything human beings can imagine, human beings can do. Positive leaders believe in the possibilities and they believe in their people. Positive leaders communicate mission, vision and values relentlessly.

Positive leaders strive to become totally dispensable to their organization. They do this by empowering their people and in the process they become invaluable.

The world needs you and you can do it. Not only can you make a difference, you are the difference!

# About the Author

A former Chief Operating Officer of a distribution and inventory management firm, Mel Hawkins has also served as a juvenile probation officer, Court Executive of a unified trial court, manager of a multi-specialty group medical practice, management and leadership consultant, and a small business owner. This experience has given Mr. Hawkins a unique perspective, one that has served him well as an innovator and problem-solver.

Educated at Manchester College where he received a BA degree, the author has also earned a Master of Science in Education (Psychology) from the University of Saint Francis and a Master of Public Affairs from Indiana University.

Mel resides with his wife in Fort Wayne, Indiana. Mel and Chris have three adult children and two grandchildren.

Active in his community, Mr. Hawkins attended Leadership Fort Wayne; has served as president and member of the Board of Managers of Byron Health Center, a 500-bed long term care facility; was a co-founder and board member of the Boys and Girls Club of Fort Wayne; co-founder, board member, and former president of the South Side Business Group of Fort Wayne and Allen County. Mel has also served on the board of the Martin Luther King Montessori School, the Alumni Board of Leadership Fort Wayne, and as co-chair of the legislative committee of the Indiana Correctional Association.

In the last five years Mel has been allocating and ever-increasing portion of his time to writing. An experienced public speaker, Mel looks forward to the opportunity to promote one of his books.

Other work by the Mel Hawkins that are available through Amazon.com or the Author's website at www.melhawkinsandassociates.com includes:

- *Radical Surgery: Reconstructing the American Health Care System,* 1stBooks Library, Bloomington, IN, July, 2002. Website is www.melhawkinsandassociate.com

- *Light and Transient Causes,*© a novel

- *Re-Inventing Education, Hope, and the American Dream: The Challenge for Twenty-first Century America.*©

Also check out the author's blogs:

THE LEADer©, (Thinking Exponentially: Leadership, Education, and the American Dream) at www.melhawkinsandassociates.com a blog that will offer articles on leadership, education, healthcare, and restoring faith and hope in the American dream to the millions of Americans who have become disenfranchised and who no longer believe they can exert control over the outcomes in their lives.

*The Positive Leadership Blog* at www/melhawkinsandassociates.com is committed to sharing the principles of positive leadership to men and women who are prospective or current leaders, whether or not they occupy formal leadership roles. The premise is that through the application of the principles of positive leadership we each have the power to change our lives and the world around us. *The Positive Leadership Blog is meant to be an interactive companion to the book The Difference is You: Power Through Positive Leadership.*

www.ingramcontent.com/pod-product-compliance
Lightning Source LLC
Chambersburg PA
CBHW051638170526
45167CB00001B/236